MY SOUL SHALL

MAKE HER Boast IN THE LORD

40 days & 40 nights of confidence building

Felicia Grayer

Dedication

I dedicate this book to my parents, Jesse and Daisy Glover, my siblings and my love balm husband Aaron.

Mom and Dad, you were so strong while facing so many of life's obstacles. I constantly think back on the wisdom given to me as a child, a teenager, and as an adult. I'll never forget all the wisdom and love showed to me in your special way. To dad in heaven; I can still hear you cheering me on!

My parents gave my siblings and me many jewels of wisdom coming up in our household. But there's one thing that I cherish about my upbringing. In observation of our family, my sisters and brother agreed to never hold grudges against each other. I suppose we found the secret to forgiveness with each other long before I discovered its healing properties for my own life. Truth and honesty were our portions, and we've kept up with it through the years. We have one of the most cohesive sibling relationships that I've ever experienced. I constantly meet families all the time with that missing piece of glue known as forgiveness. I'm so grateful.

Last, thank you to my wonderful husband Aaron, whom I affectionately refer to as my real-life Teddy Bear, for the encouragement; especially those twenty-second hugs. Thank you for motivating me during this entire process. Aaron, you have loved me back to a healthy space. Getting to live with my best friend is something that I will cherish and appreciate you for as long as I live. I love you sugar!

Table of Contents

Table of Contents

Table of Contents

Foreword

Felicia Grayer is a mighty woman of God with the hand of God on her life. I've known her nearly a decade and a half. I've had the opportunity to see her evolve into the vessel of God that she has become. This devotional will aid you in becoming a more confident individual. You will understand that God was at His best when He made you. He didn't make a mistake. You will discover that you have value. I celebrate Felicia Grayer for the impact that she is making in the Body of Christ and the world at large.

Bishop Carl D. Parrott
Rhema Word Restoration Ministries, Columbia, SC

Preface

I'm certainly no better than anyone else. I'd experienced a life of heartbreak, brokenness, and/or trauma just as much as the next person. Like most others, I didn't always appropriate the weight of such strongholds correctly. Until one day I had an epiphany! Do you know what an epiphany is? An epiphany is an "Aha" moment. I desperately needed an "Aha" moment to realize my own hope of being, becoming, and believing that I could truly be whole emotionally. My moment of epiphany came the moment that I became tired of living a life of defeat; accepting this to be the norm.

Epiphany -

> …A moment of revelation, a discovery or realization; an "*Aha*" moment that serves as an eye opener.

My turning point, or *epiphany*, was spiritual exhaustion. I'd come to the end of my own strength. I could no longer carry the weight of my own emotional mis-management. I wanted to be free. I finally wanted it. I believed in wholeness for others. Unfortunately, I never accepted it for myself. God has done the miraculous in my life. I finally believed in it for myself, as I'd believed for others in ministry. So many accept God's truth for others and not for themselves. I pray that my journey will inspire others to be honest with God and themselves so that their own emotional healing can finally begin.

-Elder Felicia Grayer
The Healed Soul Life Foundation

Introduction

In my life's journey, I've found that a lack of confidence is a complete time waster. The intent of this wonderful book is to share my testimony since God delivered me from the unconfident woman that I was. I'm originally from Brooklyn, New York, raised in the southern parts of Santee, South Carolina. I now live in Atlanta, GA. There is so much to say of my journey. However, the tools I will focus on in this book are the very keys that God gave me back in April 2014. In my life, I told God while preaching; I was tired of being oblivious to knowing how to have a confident posture. I'd been through quite a bit until this point and had lost my way. I fought with low self-esteem, depression, & anxiety, but was in grave denial. As a clergy member, sometimes we tend to focus on others more than we do ourselves. And while I was happy in my God given assignments, I was neglecting my own emotional imprisonment. I didn't take the necessary steps to move toward healing an unconfident nature. I presented God with the problems as it relates to others, but I failed in allowing God to fix my internal problems. God showed me how I lost confidence at an early age. I'd been told from Pre-K all the way until college that my skin color was unacceptable, being dark-skinned. On top of all that, I additionally dealt with relationship heartbreaks, church hurt, and just life. Unfortunately, I subconsciously believed the enemies' lies, and I created this pseudo confidence. But no longer! I walk in the truest of confidence! My journey to confidence has begun. It's time to share what I've learned. It's my prayer that you'll enjoy.

Day 1 – Boast in Discovering your Authentic self

How can I appreciate or love me better? God gave me 40 days and 40 nights to rebuild my confidence, and I was totally up for the challenge. I started to not love me so many years ago that low self-esteem was literally my comfort zone!

God graced me in "empathy" but I didn't use this grace for my life at all. It was a strength that I was mishandling unknowingly. I practiced applying empathy to EVERY situation! My business and my personal relationships and affairs needed to include empathy intentionally.

Authentic -

…Being true to an original of undisputed origin; genuine. True to one's character, spirit, or personality.

Empathy was who I was. I was empathy & empathy was me! It didn't matter what anyone else had compared to me. My authenticity was and is UNDISPUTED! This means that nothing or no one could call into question my existence or argue that my own uniqueness is unacceptable. God, without a doubt, created me to be eternally UNDISPUTED! I was so grateful that God showed me what I should have already known! Day 1 was a joyous start to my 40 day/night journey!

Here's the lesson God gave me for Day 1:

"Never forget to be yourself, authentically using your personal super power. The essence, origin of who you are. is undisputed! Who's will argue or contest God about your authenticity? No one."

Night 1 - Boast in God's idea of Justice

The first night of my 40 days and 40 nights of confidence, God took me to Psalms 34. I'd heard this chapter read devotionally in church for many, many years. Never did I once think to consider the meaning of verse two of this wonderful chapter regarding the healing of my own soul.

Psalms 34:2 KJV says,
2 "My soul shall make her boast in the Lord: the humble shall hear thereof and be glad."

This was the first scripture God led me to regarding my own personal miracle of confidence. My soul needed to heal before she could boast about anything. This first night caused me to focus on all the pain that I'd endured that led me to being this unconfident person. While searching my soul, I was so unforgiving; I bottled it up within me. Holding so tightly to the not realizing my knack to not forgive, I didn't believe that I would never be a more confident me. I needed my soul to be free of the hurt, and all the pain associated with my past. I allowed this to happen by holding unnecessary grudges.

It was completely my choice not to forgive. I believed that I was okay. I believed that everything was all right with me. It wasn't all right, and I wasn't okay. I had to forgive. My soul couldn't boast in anything because my unforgiveness imprisoned it. I wasn't able to boast in the lord without the freedom of my soul. How deep is that!?

I loved God, but I wasn't keeping the command to forgive certain people. My boasting posture was void if I couldn't be humble enough to forgive. My first nightly devotion was easier said than done. But then, God showed me the following scripture, and it pricked my very heart to forgive.

Jeremiah 9:24 AMP says,
24 "…but let him who boasts, boast in this, that he
understands and knows me, that I am the Lord who practices
lovingkindness, justice, and righteousness on the earth, for
in these things I delight," says the Lord!"

I chose my pain over God's vengeance. I never intended for vengeance to be his. Not forgiving was just like saying to God he's not capable of justice, so I'll handle it! My soul couldn't boast until I allowed God to handle this part of me, so I too could practice steadfast love, justice, and righteousness through my forgiveness. The quicker I forgave, the faster I regained confidence that I needed to love myself again.

When folks did me wrong, it translated to "I deserved it". Although, I verbalized that I didn't deserve these things happening to me; deep down inside, I justified deserving the travesties brought against me. I believed that I was less than because of what anyone had done to me. I believed I was guilty even in my innocence; because I'd always assumed that the opinions of others were truth as it concerned me.

Here's the lesson God gave me for Night 1:

"Learn justice, love and righteousness the way God intended it. This way you will truly boast godly confidence in the Lord"

Day 2 – Boast in what you Already Know to be True

We often say that we don't need the validation of others. However, there is a such thing as healthy validation from those who truly care about us. The first thing to note here is to be sure to listen carefully. Listen to the positive and negative feedback from your family, friends, and enemies. Let it sink in. Pull the feedback apart in your private time with God and the Holy Spirit will guide you into the truths that you need to accept about yourself. Then let those truths heal you and then point you towards becoming better. For years, I was so afraid of being hurt. Sometimes I subconsciously didn't listen to criticism. It felt like an attack. I guarded myself. Sometimes warranted. But now, looking back, sometimes not warranted. It's okay to guard yourself, but do so at the right time. Don't become so guarded that you miss the healthy criticism that may carry you to your next place of maturity because it doesn't feel like positive feedback. God explained to me that sometimes approval looks like disapproval. Wow! He said that sometimes the critique is coming from someone that really cares about you. If they held their criticism from you, it would be a disapproval. Because they didn't affirm you with the proper advice, you couldn't see how to grow & be better. While "Yes" people are comforting and encouraging, "No" people can help you think more critically about yourself and promote better decisions. The way I perceived opinions was causing me to put everyone's critique in the same box. Instead of discerning the good parts and then digesting them, my pain made me throw it all away. Guarding yourself at all times from a place of pain will keep you from the healthy validation or healthy critique of the people that really care about you. Be sure that your listening filters life's negative experiences or someone else's former infliction against you. The great thing about accepting God's help in healing is knowing; He sent the Holy Spirit to comfort you. God is ever present by his spirit. When I am confused about the opinions of others, whether family or friends, the comforter always reminds me to not jump to conclusions before becoming defensive.

<u>Here's the lesson God gave me for Day 2</u>:

"Remain confident in what you already know, while accepting healthy validation and/or critique from others."

He reminds us all to remain confident in what we already know to be true. Being heartbroken can sometimes cause your filter to be broken when discernment is needed. Just like the shell of a turtle stands to protect it against the outside elements, in this same manner, my brokenness kept me hidden from wholesome advice. With the Holy Spirit in constant operation, he always calmed me down when I assumed the worst in my perceptions of others and their opinions. Thank God for his Holy Spirit that teaches and comforts at all times.

John 16:13 AMP says,

13 "But when He, the Spirit of Truth, comes, He will guide you into all the truth [full and complete truth]. For He will not speak on His own initiative, but He will speak whatever He hears [from the Father—the message regarding the son], and He will disclose to you what is to come [in the future]."

Night 2 – Boast in Healthy Validation

On night two, I asked God in this moment how to fix my filter of pain so I could correctly hear what others said to me. My battle of colorism caused me to see fifty percent of received criticism, as if it came from those kids who bullied me all those years ago because of my skin color. Because I believed those opinions concerning my skin color, I took conviction as condemnation. What a sigh of relief for me. I was finally understanding my pain! I was condemning myself by using my pain as the filter that interpreted anything I heard. This was another "light bulb" moment for me! Finally, figuring out that there is a such thing as healthy validation, was a huge step for me. I didn't want to take advantage of Jesus' bloodshed for me by not listening to the Holy Spirit in those moments where I felt so condemned; I was only being offered conviction to correct myself. In reflection, I had so many of those moments. My entire life's response and/or reflex was built around my pain. In accepting healthy validation, I learned that conviction will always lead you back to Christ; but condemnation will lead you back to your guilt and magnify your past sins. To fix my filter, I needed to keep the cross of Christ at the forefront of my mind's eye so I could properly interpret all critique, disapproval, and/or rejection. Everything is not about your pain. Everyone is not out to get you. Healthy validation from the people we come in contact with, or the people we know will sometimes look like condemnation. But it's so key to listen to the Holy Spirit in the moments we feel attacked. He's always talking. Be sure to remove the filter of hurt and rejection so you can take in all that God intends to give to us through the critique of others.

God is working on all of us. The Holy Spirit is always, always illuminating the way with the word of God in our personal journeys by speaking to us. I just needed to take myself off the throne of my mind so I could listen to the Holy Spirit. God is so absolute in his mercy towards us all, even when we unknowingly reject him because of life's challenges.

I definitely needed the mercy of God on this journey. There was nothing hidden from the Holy Spirit. It's so amazing that the famed, still, small voice is always there, even when we choose not to listen to it! God sent the Holy Spirit to light the way. However, if we choose our own wisdom over the Holy Spirit's, we will gain continual heartache. God desires us to be saved and delivered from our erroneous thinking. Night two's evening scriptures reflects this.

Psalms 139:7-10 MSG says,

7 "Is there any place I can go to avoid your spirit? To be out of your sight?

8 If I climb to the sky, you're there! If I go underground , you're there!

9 If I flew on morning's wings to the far western horizon,

10 you'd find me in a minute. You're already there waiting!"

Here's the lesson God gave me for Night 2:

"In the moments that we need the proper discernment, God's voice is always there to comfort and to guide us so we can react properly to the critique, opinions, or disapproving advice of others."

Day *3* – Boast in your God-given identity

Did you know that it's okay to believe in yourself? Faith in God foremost. But also, belief in your relationship with yourself is much more powerful than you can ever imagine. Getting to know yourself is the most important thing to explore with God as an adult. Have faith in God's identity for your life; but also have faith in you being good enough… Let God share what he sees you as, then have faith in that... You are here for a purpose. Find it. Pursue it. Believe it. Faith it. Confide in your purpose. It won't let you down.

I wish I'd learned years ago that it was okay to believe in myself. That's not how my mind was setup about 20 years ago. Believing in myself depended upon finding my identity in God; not just as a preacher, but I needed to know the actual message that God wanted to speak through me. I was here for a purpose. I knew I was to be a preacher. I accepted the call to preach after a few years of running because I was in so much emotional pain. I couldn't understand why God would call someone like me who was so damaged!

It turns out that once I began in ministry; I loved helping the poor in spirit, and the broken-hearted. My empathetic nature was always on 1,000. I enjoyed working with the people of God so much while helping them heal spiritually. This was IT! I found my niche as a preacher! At 14 years old, God always referred to me as little weeping Prophetess. My favorite prophet in the bible at the time was Jeremiah. As I got to know who I was in God, the identity revealed my ministry involving prophetic mediation; birthed by the empathy gained from my childhood trauma. Empathy was the same tool I used to put myself in someone else's shoes so I could feel what they were feeling. Besides feeling what they felt, I was so open to seeing people through the eyes of God so I could prophetically mediate through the gifts of the Holy Spirit. I used heavily, identified as an introvert. However, God took me to the Beatitudes one day to study Matthew 5:2-11. There was a mystery that the Holy Spirit wanted to reveal to me! He said even though you use the introvert scale to identify yourself; I want you to view the Beatitudes as God-approved personalities. At that moment, I didn't understand. He shared with me that all my life, I'd saw God in others constantly. I did this to a fault. However, as I read the Beatitudes, God asked me if I saw myself among these personas as it related to my own spirit. My entire countenance lit up when I got to verse 8!

Matthew 5:8 AMP says,

8 Blessed are the pure in heart, for they will see God."

Wow! God showed me myself in verse 8! What an amazing revelation! All I knew was the Holy Spirit in me agreed with this, not so obvious mystery. I'd unknowingly been exhibiting this beatitude my entire life. My "GOD" identity was a "PURE IN HEART"! It was a treasure hidden in me that took me a while to find. I'm so blessed that God opened my eyes to this. Now I could be confident of who I was now that I KNOW who that IS! I allowed God be the captain of my soul and he was sailing me away from the hurt that wouldn't let me see my true identity. For that, I'm grateful!

<u>**Here's the lesson God gave me for Day 3:**</u>

"God not only cares about us knowing who he is after we pursue him, he also cares about who we think we are. Your identity is so hidden in God that you must get so close to him to find yourself. Go so deep in relationship with him that you ignore the parts of your soul that tells you that you're someone other than what God says."

In Matthew 16, Peter's identity revealed while he fellow-shipped with Jesus, after he recognized who he was. Jesus was looking for them to acknowledge him by describing who they thought he was. Peter quickly spoke up.

Matthew 16:13-18 AMP says,

13 "…He asked His disciples, "Who do people say that the Son of Man is?

14 And they answered, some say John the Baptist: others, Elijah; and still others, Jeremiah, or {just} one of the prophets."

15 He said to them, "But who do you say that I am?"

16 Simon Peter replied, "You are the Christ (the Messiah, the Anointed), the Son of the living God."

17 Then Jesus answered him, "Blessed [happy, spiritually secure, favored by God] are you, Simon son of Jonah, because flesh and blood (mortal man) did not reveal this to you, but My Father who is in heaven.

18 And I say to you that you are Peter, and on this rock, I will build my church; and the gates of death will not overpower it.

It wasn't until after Peter followed Jesus and properly acknowledged him, did Jesus reveal his GOD-identity!

Night *3* – Boast in being a Joint-Savior of the world

My day ended with this thought, "Follow Jesus, acknowledge his identity, and he'll show you your own identity. Thinking that I was already close enough to God; this thought process was when I slipped. I was able to acknowledge who the Son of God was with all the honor I could muster. However, I was always very fearful to get close enough to God to search out the totality of my identity. Not just my place in ministry, but my place of purpose. My place away from pain.

Peter would never perceive that Jesus was the Son of God if he hadn't fellowship with him during the most difficult times. He would've never have known his future's value if he hadn't listened for Jesus's response to his acknowledgement of him. I acknowledged God, and I even heard when he called me to preach. But brothers and sisters, there was so much more to my identity that I hadn't even fathomed!

I found that following Jesus, acknowledging Jesus, and accepting his identity for your life was another formula that would help me get to know my personal God-given identity. For those of you saved for a short time, or a long time, be sure that you understand that your identity is a constant; but is always at the mercy of God's will for your life. The further you go in your relationship with Jesus, it will reveal more of your God-identity unto you! Always remember that God is in control entirely. He is faithful to finish the work of his son in you if you let him.

Jesus was not only savior of the world and fisherman of men. He created the blueprint for having the courage to walk in our own God-given identity just as he did! Jesus was the Son of the living God. However, he was also savior of the world. He naturally identified as Prince of heaven, but he freed us as the Prince of Peace! He became the savior of the world through death!

So it was with Peter! Peter wasn't just a disciple; he became so much closer to Jesus! Don't allow pain and anguish to become your identity. Let God in so that he can share your own treasured identity with you; given at conception. The closer you get to God, the more you will see yourself the way he sees you.

<u>Here's the lesson God gave me for Night 3:</u>
"Just like Jesus, we are all supposed to be submitting our will to him so that WE can help SAVE THE WORLD too! As joint-heirs with Christ, we are now all joint-saviors with him! You can save the world! Yes, you! Your pain, like Jesus' pain, has purpose; and it all ties to the identity and the purpose that God has for you. He didn't call you to be ordinary in a world that needs extraordinary people to do the will of God. Your God-given identity matters"

There's an identity for you that is so hidden in God, he is literally playing hide and seek until we find out who we are in him. God wants you to come find him. In the process? You'll find your true self. We can only find identity in God. Find out what your purpose in this world is by going after God. You're never too old to find him and yourself! Personality and Purpose shouldn't be the fickle and indecisive points in your life. The first step to living your true self recognizes who God is through Jesus Christ. In seeking the identity of God, God

21

will then show us who we are. Created to do good works; we should always endeavor to take the journey that God has set for our lives. Our trials, trauma, and pain are like traffic signs pointing the way to our purpose. No trial, no heartache, no trauma comes without purpose.

Ephesians 2:10 AMP says,

13 For we are His workmanship [His own master work, a work of art], created in Christ Jesus [reborn from above, spiritually transformed, renewed, ready to be used] for good works, which God prepared [for us] beforehand [taking paths which He set], so that we would walk in them [living the good life which he prearranged and made ready for us]."

Let's not forget this popular scripture…
Roman 8:28 AMP says,

28 "And we know [with great confidence] that God [who is deeply concerned about us] causes all things to work together [as a plan] for good for those who love God, to those who are called according to His plan and purpose."

God chose you for the purpose of gracing the world with your *presence*. Whatever you've gone through, or will go through? It's meant for *good*. Always remember that the end of the story is a happy ending, predestined to be ours when Jesus denied himself and took up his own cross. Be a *living testimony*. Be a *testament*. Pass the *test*. Go *save* the *world*.

Savior -

…a person who rescues someone from danger or harm.

Day 4 – Boast in God's unchanging Opinion of you

You are Great because GOD made you to be just that! Believe it! Love who he made you to be and become. To love you, you must love the you that God sees. It's become a cliché in some sense to say, "I want to see me the way God sees me". Here's the sore thumb or throbbing thought that will get you to seeing yourself the way God does. God's opinion is king. Let his opinion of you take a proper place on the throne of your mind. You can never see yourself through the eyes of God if you consistently base your self-worth on the way others see you. I'd perfected seeing others through the eyes of God. Meanwhile, I neglected seeing myself through the same lens that I was so passionate about having for others! I finally realized that I deserved a little empathy too. In fact, God had been trying to show me this same empathy. He wanted me to run to his arms and heal the part of my soul that still needed deliverance. I needed to accept God's unconditional love for me, his empathy towards me and his undeniable peace. God's sovereignty and his person makes him GREAT and greatly to be praised. We define sovereignty as supreme power or authority. While God didn't give humankind supreme power, he gave us authority. God takes pride in how he created mankind. The Holy Spirit comforted me by teaching me that it is this same authority that I wasn't accepting in my mind's eye for myself. I needed to view myself as God's wonderful creation. But I also needed to understand that humankind's sovereignty is in the authority given to us by God. Although we are not beings of deity, it's the authority given to us that makes us special. This was the first thing that I needed to realize; to love me the way God did.

The second thing was to accept the fashion in which he made me as an individual soul. To do this, I needed to go to Genesis 1:26-27.

Genesis 1:26-27 AMP says,

26 *"Then God said, "Let us (Father, Son, Holy Spirit) make man in our image, according to our likeness [not physical, but a spiritual personality and moral likeness]; and let them have complete authority over the fish of the sea, the birds of the air, the cattle, and over the earth."*

27 *So God created man in his own image, in the image and likeness of God, he created them."*

God, Elohim, the creator, consulted with himself before he created his greatest masterpiece! You and I! He had to pause for a moment before creating his greatest & most treasured creation; mankind! In Genesis 1, before he even creates the flesh, God perfectly fashioned our souls in his image, or in his likeness. God's personality, or the soul of us, is the driving force in our lives even when we don't realize it. What we need to love ourselves and others? God instilled it in us at the foundation of the world.

What does that mean? God creates human souls with the same seven attributes that he has! We flourish in our God-given personality as humans when we operate in these areas daily!

They are:

1. Mercy

2. Goodness.

3. Grace.

4. Holiness.

5. Righteousness.

6. Justice

7. Love.

After studying these phenomenal attributes, I measure myself according to these standards. I'm talking about standards sealed and affirmed within me by God himself! Therefore, seeing myself the way God sees me is so important. The closer we get to God, it's easier to display these attributes naturally. They're already a part of our soul's make up. The will of God were all set on the pedestal of our soul until satan tricked mankind into believing against the word of God. If Adam and Eve hadn't listened to the opinion of the devil, there would be no intro of iniquity as we know it. We could all be better if we learn from Adam's mistake and live because our creator's opinion is all that matters. He's the one who created us. After understanding how he feels about me, and what he put inside of me; we can all look in the mirror and love ourselves the way God loves us! Remind yourself that he made you in his image. Learning to appreciate my outward appearance didn't seem that important after I understood what God saw in me. He saw his own spoken, affirmed word in my soul. In the same chapter, Genesis 1, verse 31 was a sight for sore eyes. The sweetness of this revelation lifted my countenance while reading from the amplified bible.

Genesis 1:31 AMP says,

31 "God saw everything that he had made, and behold, it was very good and he validated it completely…"

Just in case you didn't catch it yet; God validates us! Completely! The mystery isn't really a mystery at all. God created in his image. However, it takes a relationship with God so that we can truly understand who we are, how we are, and why we can love ourselves and others because of these infinite attributes embedded in our soul.

<u>Here's the lesson God gave me for Day 4:</u>

"His opinion seals and is unchanging. His spoken word created you to be phenomenal in God's likeness, with his attributes as the core of our being."

Brothers and sisters, his word never goes back void. It will always accomplish that which it set out to do! We just need to get to know ourselves as God sees us so that we can love who God made us to be.

Isaiah 55:11 AMP says,

11 "So will my word be which goes out of my mouth; It will not return unto me void (useless, without result), Without accomplishing what I desire, and without succeeding the matter for which I sent it."

Night 4 – Boast in loving God, yourself, and others

Iniquity can shape our lives so much that we sometimes become blinded to the greatness that God himself put inside of us all. There are no exceptions. We are all exceptional because we're created in his image. Always remember that he spake it to be so, and it is so. So now, my personal progress continues with me saying and believing that, "I am exceptional". Not because I'm so great and wonderful in my own eyes. I am great and wonderfully made because God spoke it to be; before the beginning of my time on this earth. I am his masterpiece, his treasure and his proud accessory. He's proud of who I already am because he ensured that my soul reflects his image. His word in me never boomerangs back to him. It's an eternal constant. God loves me, and there's truly nothing that I can do about it. He also expects me to love me. But last, he intends that we love others with the same sentiment that he loves us. In simple terms, we're created to first love God, & love our neighbor.

Here's the lesson God gave me for Night 4:

"God created us as relational beings. He calls us to be in relationship with him while also in right relationship with our neighbor. Loving God and our neighbor the right way produces a love for ourselves while giving us a sense of belonging and community the way God intended."

I asked God three questions, but also learned three things I learned to love who God made me in his image. Let's look briefly at what God placed on my heart:

Why do we move & have our being in him?

-Our body speaks his name and you are literally moving as a bearer of his name, I AM, THAT I AM. Every breath we take is from his spirit. Every move we make is because he fashioned us to do so exceptionally. Be sure to read Acts 17:28.

Why are we speakers of life?

-We are because God did it first! Being created in his image allows us the same power to speak life with our words. Speaking life isn't something new; done at the conception of the world. There is life and power in what we speak. Be sure to read Proverbs 18:21.

Why are we victorious in his image?

-God prepared our future. Jesus Christ's death solidified our rightful place with God if we accept him as savior. We've already won. Jesus's death decided the winners and losers; for the rest of eternity. Be sure to read I Corinthians 15:54.

God purchased us through the blood of his own son. He protected his investment by not allowing Satan to win in our lives. Don't believe Satan's lies about who you are. Don't allow guilt, the shame of sin, or trauma to dictate who you are. Love yourself through the eyes of God. God's opinion is king. You are exceptional. You are phenomenal.

Never forget how *LOVED YOU ARE...*

Day 5 – Boast Knowing that it's Working for your good

Dwelling on past hurts, and mistakes are killers of Confidence. Learn from your mistakes and hurts. Self-pity should never have a place to rest in your subconscious. Let respect for your experiences take up residence in your spirit to breed a more confident you!

While most of my testimony explains my journey to emotional healing, this book focuses solely on confidence. However, I want to explain briefly the difference between emotional and mental healing. Mental health - our ability to process information caused by life's circumstances. If you flip over this same coin, you'll see mental health's silent cousin, emotional health. Emotional healing has to do with our ability to express our feelings based on the information we've processed mentally. Many people dealing with emotional pain tend to under-process information when life happens. In the same breath while under processing, they suppress the emotions associated to a particular circumstance, event, or trauma.

What does over processing look like? If you've ever asked God "Why me?", then you probably know what it's like to dwell on the reasons anything is happening or has happened to you; you have an emotional management issue, more so than a mental issue. Over-processing leads to self-loathing, unnecessary guilt, shame, & self-pity. I needed to learn how to respect every circumstance, upset, or trauma as it was so that I could put the "Why me" in proper perspective. It's often said that there is a purpose in our pain. Even I've shared with you that your pain leads to your purpose. Somehow, even when we seek to do good, evil is always present. On my present journey, I still have to confront guilt and shame because the spirit of condemnation will always accuse me.

I would say things like, "Oh, how I wish I knew this so many years ago." But let's be fair and flip this guilt statement to an empowerment statement. Instead of saying, "I wish I knew better many years ago", I empower myself by saying, I once viewed my pain as punishment, but now I view it as my pleasurable road map that leads me to my purpose. Changing my guilt or shame statements to empowerment statements puts the proper respect on my experiences so that I could heal from emotional pain.

Here's the lesson God gave me for Day 5:

"Finding the root of the pain is just the beginning. Learn to respect it as the green light that will signal you towards that wonderful feeling of purpose; this will cause you to now appreciate what you went through."

John 3:16 AMP says,

16 "For God so [greatly] loved and dearly prized the world, that he [even] gave his [one and] only begotten son, so that whoever believes and trusts in him [as savior] shall not perish, but have eternal life.

Night 5 – Boast in Your Journey from Pain to Purpose

God said to me, "A cold happens by the brisk wind of the Winter, just as easily as the cool breeze of the Summer. The cold itself is not important, unless you learn the root cause of it so that you heal." After finding the root, present it in your private time with God so that he can show you its purpose. This is God's way. If God's only son wasn't too good to be an example of triumph over pain, then who are we? We are no better. Jesus' pain purposed to save the world. Our pain? It too has significant purpose. It's honestly not about us. It's about the eternal resolve of God's investment of freedom for the world that he loves through the blood of his son Jesus Christ. Job perfected the art of putting his circumstances into perspective.

Here's the lesson God gave me for Night 5:

"Jesus' father sent him to die! We are no better. We will all experience the journey from pain to purpose."

Your life is not your own. Just in case you've gone through, are going through now or expect to go through a unique experience? Be steadfast knowing that it will inspire others to learn from your life. God trusts us to get through the same way that his son Jesus, our savior did. Job makes an honest proclamation in Job 13:15 while he was going through.

Job 13:15 AMP says,
15 "Even though he kills me; I will hope in him. Nevertheless, I will argue my ways to his face.

Day **6** – Boast in Knowing that God Is Always There

God never promised you and I that we would never go through storms. But he did promise to always be with us. He's always in the midst of our storms, even until the ends of the earth. You are not *alone*. You can rest on his promise to always be with you! There's nothing my God cannot do! Day six built my confidence by the realization of God never leaving me!

He can do it all, including being with me or my neighbor at all times. Learning confidence by fellowship with God really took away all the loneliness and grief that I'd felt from being rejected. It also helped in those moments when family or friends went on to be with the Lord. After the death of Moses, Joshua had to come face to face with his own courage despite his temporary moment of grief. He knows a thing or two about feeling alone in the time of grief or emotional distress. God consoled Joshua by reminding him to not be alarmed or terrified because God would always be with him wherever he goes. This point of Joshua's existence was an inspirational parallel to pattern myself to.

Joshua 1:9 CEB says,
9 "I've commanded you to be brave and strong, haven't I? Don't be alarmed or terrified, because the Lord your God is with you wherever you go."

<u>**Here's the lesson God gave me for Day 6:**</u>

"Ignoring God's presence in your life will never make him leave you. He's waiting patiently for you to acknowledge him. Thereafter, he will take on your cares as his own. Your burdens will become light!"

Bearing grief and/or rejection kept me in a place of solitude. Unfortunately, I would further isolate in those moments instead of allowing God in those broken spaces in my soul. Once I learned how to invite God into my personal space of solitude, I was able to heal much faster.

Matthew 11:29-30 AMP says,

29 "Take my yoke upon you and learn of me [following me as my disciple], for I am gentle and humble in heart, and you will find rest (renewal, blessed, quiet) for your souls.
30 For my yoke is easy [to bear] and my burden is light."

Jesus' yoke is gentle and full of humility. It offers rest to the weary soul. Let Jesus trade his yoke for your burdens. It is his good pleasure to help carry your load of grief and distress because of life's challenges.

As we continue on our journey to get to know Jesus, sometimes, there will be situations that make us feel like God just isn't there. You won't feel him, see him, or hear him. This is a test of your spiritual maturity.

Night **6** – Boast in knowing that God guides us

On the evening of night six, I ran across Isaiah 30:20-21 and it literally blew me away:

Isaiah 30:20-21 AMP says,

20 "Though the Lord gives you the bread of adversity and the water of oppression, yet your Teacher will no longer hide himself, but your eyes will [constantly] see your teacher.
21 Your ears will hear a word behind you, "This is the way", walk in it, whenever you turn to the right or to the left."

When the teacher is giving an exam, he or she is quiet. So it is with God. We've all heard this scenario or parallel. It's absolute in understanding how God works. He's watching to see what you've learned. In those times that you just can't hear him, it may seem like all hell has broken loose. That's when you must stay grounded. I had to learn this when it came down to my hidden pain. That last piece of me needing repair, I assumed broken; I finally gave it to God. It became the longest exam of my life. Regarding this peculiar test, I was failing miserably, and God was silent. However, he'd already given me all the answers that I'd ever needed. There's a song called, "God in me". The God in us whispers to us along the way. Unfortunately, we aren't always listening to that still, sweet voice. The more I listened, the more magnified that voice was, it gave clarity in times of distress.

1 John 4:4 ESV says,

4 "Little children, you are from God and have overcome them, for he who is in you is greater than he who is in the world."

<u>**Here's the lesson God gave me for Night 6:**</u>

"It's in God's nature to give us what we need. He strives to get our attention through the storms of life. We just have to be sure to learn the lesson, pass the test, and build a strong confidence because we know the personality of God."

Understanding God's personality really helped me in my journey of emotional healing. There are things about God that are not negotiable. His promise to never leave you is one of those things! I went through many things in my life without surrendering them to God. I learned that it's in his nature to not only be with me, but to always be there for me.

Realizing that this is something I thought I already knew was an eye opener. Knowing and believing are two different things. Believing is such a powerful thing. Somehow, I believed this about God for others, but not for myself. Asaph said it best in his song to God in Psalm 73, verses 25 and 26.

Psalm 73:25-26 AMP says,
25 "Whom have I in heaven [but you]? And besides You, I desire nothing on earth.
26   My flesh and my heart may fail, But God is the rock and strength of my heart and my portion forever."

Learning to lean totally on God was scary for me, but it was also worth it. I became free in discovering the personality of God towards me. I fell in love with God all over again. My personal confidence was organically coming alive in me again!

Day 7 – Boast in How Special You Are

A boost of confidence comes from being the best you that you can be! Being you is under-rated. You are one of a kind. God made you in his image. There's no other you in this world. You are perfect. Progression and growth are inevitable when you strive to be the best you, you can be. I spent too much time disliking who I was. That is time that I cannot get back. The only thing that you or I could do after having this kind of low self-esteem is to rebuild thought patterns. After looking at how much God revered me and how he delicately created me; it made me want to get to know myself through God's eyes so that I could truly love me. I literally had to cast down every imagination that exalted itself against the knowledge of God. I replaced the knowledge and opinions of others with the knowledge of God. There is a scripture that I'd known for most of my life. However, I'd never needed it as it regards to my own self-esteem. Any warfare against my mind came to me in the form of lies and the opinions of others. satan began early with this weapon against me. I literally needed to cast down the evil imaginations that he caused me to believe about myself. The scripture in II Corinthians 10:5, as I understood it; had never touched me in this way until now.

2 Corinthians 10:5 AMP says,

5 "We are destroying sophisticated arguments and every exalted and proud thing that sets itself up against the [true] knowledge of God, and we are taking every thought and purpose captive to the obedience of Christ..."

The enemy worked hard to get me to believe his lies. I believed them for far too long. I soon woke up and replaced his lies with the knowledge of God! Step by step, I replaced satan's false truths with the knowledge of God; My new intent was to find scriptures that combated those lies. Psalm 139:14 is heavily quoted but it held a deeper truth that I needed to discover.

Psalm 139:14 AMP says,

14 "I will give thanks and praise to You, for I am fearfully and wonderfully made; Wonderful are Your works, and my soul knows it very well."

I was eager to research this scripture. In my study time, I found that the original Hebrew meaning for fearfully and wonderfully was: 'Fearfully means to inspire reverence or fear; to stand in awe of. Wonderfully means to be distinctly separated; to be distinguished'. Remember how God gave us authority in the earth? Yes. We were "fearfully made" to take authority in the earth. I had a power that I was refusing to use. God gave me "Power and Authority" from the beginning of time! I was back on track and felt empowered by replacing the lies of satan with the knowledge of God! The creator intended for us to be revered and looked upon in awe.

Here's the lesson God gave me for Day 7:

I learned without a doubt that my soul's confidence comes from knowing that God made distinguished and perfect as his creation. I stand out uniquely. From the inside out, I was certainly special. Not just me, we all are!

Night 7 – Boast in your YOU-niqueness

It was the last line of this scripture of Psalm 139:14, that quenched my thirst. It says, "and my soul knows it very well." What did it mean in this context for my soul to know well? Know in this context means; to learn, acknowledge, declare, admit, and/or confess. Well translates to exceedingly much, in abundance, excessive, diligent, extremely firm, and/or greatly. The 13th verse of Psalm 139 backs up this notion oh so well!!

Psalm 139:13 AMP says,

13 "For you formed my innermost parts; You knit me [together] in my mother's womb."

David's soul boasted in the God of his salvation! He boasted on how God fashioned his inner and his outer man! No arrogance, just facts! It was confidence felt in the pit of his soul! He was confident in himself because he was confident in God's creation! Himself! What an example of how a soul boasts in the Lord! David was revering the creation of his father! He was speaking the knowledge of God over the lies of satan about himself! He had a celebration in song; for who God was to him and who he was created to be! It was a celebration and knew that there was nothing he could do about it! God spoke him into existence, and he was excessively aware with gratefulness!

<u>**Here's the lesson God gave me for Night 7:**</u>

We are distinguished. Yet, we are called to be grateful to God, the father, for setting us apart in our own uniqueness and individuality. Celebrate your YOU-niqueness!

Day 8 – Boast in Forgiving Yourself and Others

Life's obstacles can impact your spirit and subconscious with fear. Don't be afraid to try again after a mistake or mishandling of decisions. There truly is a blessing in our ability to learn and grow from our mistakes. The soul records your mistakes and your victories. But the soul is sometimes unforgiving of mistakes, even after your mind has forgotten them. How do you fix this? Forgive yourself. Our soul, the spirit, and the body are all connected. In physics, the law of gravitation says that all particles of matter in the universe attract each other through the force of gravity. Just like the laws of gravity, there are things that we just can't change about how our being works. God made us a certain way. We are wired as mind, body, and soul. So, therefore, we are wired to be successful if we follow the principles that he sets forth for his people. We know forgiveness in scripture as a "Key to the Kingdom". It's a non-negotiable principle set by God himself, just as the law of gravity is indisputable. Forgiveness affects not only our soul, but our spirit and our physical bodies. When there is emotional pain embedded in our soul, we feel it in our minds and our bodies. Once I began focusing on my own forgiveness, I was lighter, and freedom flooded my soul! I felt better in my body and my mind was sharper than ever.

<u>Here's the lesson God gave me for Day 8:</u>

Forgiveness was not only for me to give to others; also, to give to myself. It will heal mind, body, & soul.

Night 8 – Boast in Letting go; Love will Point the Way

I desperately needed to forgive. It was so freely given to me by God, yet I couldn't offer it to others or myself. I discovered that because of grudges; I was more likely to have depression and anxiety due to the social issues that plagued my soul. My personality was flawed because I viewed others through the lens of my grudges. I held others accountable for the hurt that they weren't responsible for. Grudges will cloud your thinking and take away your ability to trust others the way God intended for us to. Forgiveness is an ongoing practice. It's a way of life, a way of thinking, and a way of giving. Forgiveness is God's way to not only get us into heaven, but to keep our souls cleansed from the negative emotions that we suppress in our lives; robbing our confidence.

Here's the lesson God gave me for Night 8:

To forgive, you need love. Love gives us the road map to freedom. Love keeps no record of wrong. You can extend the power of forgiveness to others and yourself with the power of love.

1 Corinthians 13:5 AMP says,

5 "It is not rude; it is not self-seeking; it is not provoked [nor overly sensitive and easily angered]; it does not take into account a wrong endured."

This verse pointed the way so that I could forgive while loving my neighbor as myself, as it says in Mark 12:31. Go read it, my friends! It will bless you. Besides, it's the second commandment given to us by Jesus himself.

Day **9** – Boast in God-given Vision for your life

Emotional pain kept me from my purpose and my true identity. My life just didn't seem to go in the right direction. Asking God why doesn't always provide the answer when we are seemingly on the wrong path. He is waiting for us to share every moment of our life's aspirations with him. His delight is in our asking him what's next. Belief in his purpose for your life, will clear your vision so that you can plainly write the vision, and pursue according to his will. Just ask him to give you clear vision. Don't forget to listen carefully. Listen, write, believe, & pursue! I didn't always have confidence, being so focused on the burdens of my soul.

One highlight of this book is to point you toward a rewarding relationship with God. This relationship will reward you with the confidence that you need for life's challenges. Here's what I learned on the ninth day of my journey:

Here's the lesson God gave me for Day 9:

Your relationship with God will reveal his vision for your life. The closer you get to know him, the more he will give your life direction. He knows you better than you will ever know yourself.

Having to admit that my own personal relationship with God wasn't where it should be, was humbling. It was the honest push of truth that I needed to heal.

Night 9 – Boast in knowing God's Will

His plan and purpose aren't always attractive, but it is worth it! I love reading the different witnessing accounts of the bible from the men and women of God. Being obedient to his will for your life can be difficult if you are insensitive to the personality of God. Knowing a bit about how God operates will give you confidence when you are weathering an impossible storm!

I found that obedience became relatively easy when I understood the ways of God. When I understood that every circumstance and situation in my life was working toward God's purpose, I became at ease with trusting him with my life. It was the peace of God that made my trying times worth living. Peace gives the assurance that I'm in the will of God.

Isaiah 46:10 AMP says,

10 "Declaring the end and the result from the beginning, and from ancient times the things which have not [yet] been done, Saying, 'My purpose will be established, And I will do all that pleases me and fulfills MY purpose,"

Here's the lesson God gave me for Night 9:

God's will dictates my life; that dictation connects to someone else's purpose. Being in the will of God will work not only for my good, but for the good of someone else's life.

Day 10 – Boast in using Godly Responses of Hope

Regret? Or Renewed hope? You choose. Responding wisely to life's obstacles gives a confident outlook of hope. Don't let regret steal your ability to renew hope. Always respond wisely. My response to life needed a new glimpse of hope. I lost hope in me and I needed to get it back. I couldn't see myself as healthy or whole. I couldn't see myself as successful in life. I couldn't see myself in a loving relationship. I couldn't imagine a life purposed by God. I had no hope that I'd accomplish anything at all. When you don't see things getting better, you tend to lose hope. One thing was for sure when I started this journey in 2014. I didn't want to live a life filled with regret any longer. I needed to take my life back with renewed hope. I needed to believe through hope again for my life, not just for others. No more regrets. It's all in how I responded to my life's circumstances. My response should always deliver hope at every turn. I was ready to hope again. I needed to reset my hope. I needed to reboot my belief. Not only in my God-given purpose for me, but I needed to renew belief in myself.

Here's the lesson God gave me for Day 10:

Our response to life's circumstances should always breed hope without regret. Believe that God's plan is far bigger than we could ever imagine. Seeing hope through to completion in life gives us victory on the other side of all of our suffering. Hope leads the way.

Night **10** – Boast in Never Losing Hope

I realized by this time that my hope was hiding in my heart; under lock and key. I was reluctant to give it freely. Hope was an automatic obtained by my salvation. In prayer, the Holy Spirit encouraged me to put the totality of my hope in him to comfort me at all times. I assumed that extending myself again would waste my hope. My disbelief of hope's sanctity robbed me of pure hope in God. I needed to define my personal hope again.

Hope -

 ...a feeling of expectation and desire for a
 certain thing to happen.

Here's the lesson God gave me for Night 10:

Don't lose your hope. God will never waste your belief in him. He will never waste your hope in him. You can unlock your hope towards God. The truest of confidence depends on it.

Proverbs 13:12 AMP says,

12 "Hope deferred makes the heart sick, but when desire is fulfilled, it is a tree of life."

I allowed my heartbreak to rob me of my hope. Sometimes I just didn't know any better. Now that I know better, I keep my hope in God. I trust and believe that God's plan will supersede any emotional or distressing circumstance that comes my way. I learned to believe again that God would give me the desires of my heart according to his will.

Day 11 – Boast in Living well by Responding well

Some things aren't as deep as they seem. Rejection, verbal abuse, disrespect, etc., is sometimes intended to take you down mentally and emotionally. Don't give these antics too much power over you. You're tougher than you appear! Soon, everyone will know how tough you really are! I was strong in my living, but not strong in my responses. I had consecration and sanctification on lock. However, my ability to respond properly according to the proper application of scripture was weak. I lived well, *so I thought*, but failed in response to life.

<u>**Here's the lesson God gave me for Day 11:**</u>

Live well. Respond well. If you live well before God, don't forget to respond well while connecting with your neighbor. Your true strength is shown in how well you respond to the antics of others.

Living for God can feel isolate without proper response to life's circumstances. Living well and/or responding well is as equally important to my walk with God and/or my neighbor. Proper response would save the world from unnecessary emotional distress if we knew how to use it. My elderly mentors often say that "no response is a response". Jesus was the example for us to learn a proper response.

Isaiah 53:7 AMP says,

7 "He was oppressed and he was afflicted. Yet, he did not open his mouth [to complain or defend himself]; Like a lamb to the slaughter, and like a sheep that is silent before her shearers, so he did not open his mouth."

Night 11 – Boast in Responding like Jesus did

It opened my eyes the more I journeyed to healing; it was easy to not only respond to others, but how to forgive others like Jesus did. Jesus made it look so easy! Being Christ-like was another key to my confidence for responding properly to the opinions of others.

Luke 23:34 AMP says,

34 "…and Jesus was saying, "Father, forgive them; for they do not know what they are doing." And they cast lots, dividing his clothes among themselves."

When we follow Christ, we are to take on a certain likeness that should closely parallel the actions and reactions of Jesus as presented in scripture. The phrase, "I want to be like Jesus" was a cliché that I didn't take serious in every area of my life. I had a desire to mimic some of his ways, but not with everything. I needed to whole-heartedly give myself over to being like Jesus.

Here's the lesson God gave me for Night 11:

We should grow in our imitation of Christ. Being falsely accused will push you to a necessary mode of solitude to gain better clarity, through progressive love for God. Confidence is a benefit.

Paul, the Apostle said,

I Corinthians 11:1 AMP says,

1 "Imitate me, just as I imitate Christ."

Day 12 – Boast in Knowing You're Important to God

Sometimes, because we can't see God, we can easily assume that he doesn't care. The truth of the matter is this. If God cares for the sparrows, will he not take care of you or I? You are important! Somehow, I thought that thinking that I was important crossed the line to arrogance. We don't entertain our importance because of fear of being too arrogant about how we feel about ourselves. It's ok to have confidence because we are important! I used to be afraid to think or feel that I was important. I feared thinking too deceitfully about myself. The elders taught me to stay humble. However, I was so humble that I allowed the thoughts of unimportance to take over my mind and control me.

<u>Here's the lesson God gave me for Day 12:</u>

Every living thing is important to God.

Matthew 10:29-31 AMP says,

29 "Are not two little sparrows sold for a copper coin? And yet not one of them falls to the ground apart from your father's will.
30 But even the very hairs of your head are all numbered [for the Father is sovereign and has complete knowledge].
31 So do not fear; you are more valuable than many sparrows."

Learning how to balance my humility and/or confidence and the understanding of my importance to God was like changing clothes. I needed to strip off all the bad thoughts about myself and change into something more confident. It was a welcomed exchange! We are individually important to God!

Night 12 – Boast in Valuing Others the Way God does

Did you know that being evil doesn't keep you from receiving provisions from God? Regardless of how we treat God, the father, it's still his pleasure to provide for us even in our most unlovable states.

Matthew 5:44-45 AMP says,

44 "But I say to you, love [that is, unselfishly seek the best or higher good for] your enemies and pray for those who persecute you,

45 so that you may [show yourself to] be the children of your Father who is in heaven; for He makes his sun rise on those who are evil and those who are good, and makes the rain fall on the righteous [those who are morally upright] and the unrighteous [the unrepentant, those who oppose him]."

Understanding how important we all are will provide the backdrop for healing in this world between races or genders. It certainly made for a more confident view of *people* in my mind.

Here's the lesson God gave me for Night 12:

We are to value all living things just as God does…

This is spiritual maturity at his best. How do I match this set value of importance towards my neighbor? It was a side effect to understanding how important everyone is to God. It doesn't matter to God that some have rejected him. He still allows them to feel the sunshine upon their skin and the rain to beat upon their head. So, it is as I learned to value all of God's creations.

Day **13** – Boast in Knowing You're a Work of Art

Somewhere in the world there is someone who wishes they had your hair, your eyes, & your smile. I know someone convinced you of how unacceptable you are. You are just right for your Goldilocks, or whoever the real-life admirer in your life is. They're ready to eat your porridge, or sleep in your bed.

Ephesians 2:10 AMP says,

10a…"For we are his workmanship [his own master work, a work of art]…"

When I think of art, I think of anything that is precious, priceless, and timeless. There's no set standard for beauty in the art world. Beauty is in the eye of the beholder. In the eye of the creator, we are all beautiful. Every blessing of good looks or opportunities have come into fruition because he allowed it.

<u>Here's the lesson God gave me for Day 13:</u>

We are his masterpieces. As his wonderful works of art, God created us to live a life of good works regardless physical looks.

Ephesians 2:10b AMP says,

10b "…created in Christ Jesus [reborn from above-spiritually transformed, renewed, ready to be used] for good works, which God prepared [for us] beforehand [taking paths which he set], so that we would walk in them [living the good life which he prearranged and made ready for us]."

Night **13** – Boast in the Good life God has for you

Be grateful. Thank God for all of your blessings, good looks, and opportunities. God cares more about the adorning of our inner man. As our creator, God wants us to be confident in who he created us to be. Ephesians 2:10 is a favorite of mine. I want to do good works. I want to live the good life predestined by God and made ready for me.

<u>Here's the lesson God gave me for Night 13:</u>

This is where true confidence lies. Being able to trust God's plan for your life? For all of our lives? That's most important. Believe in the will of God for yourself and others. We can live the good life.

As humans, we tend to want to know the plan or purpose so that we can have a sense of control. Therefore, we focus so much on the vanity of our physical bodies. We can't control our aging, so we try to control our God-given purpose. We need godly understanding and wisdom to live the good life by doing good works. We need to believe this principle for ourselves and others. Only the Holy Spirit can help us with the discernment that we need to *connect* with others to live a good life and do good works *together*.

Proverbs 3:5-6 AMP says,

5 "Trust in and rely confidently on the Lord with all your heart and do not rely on your own insight or understanding.
6 In all your ways know and acknowledge and recognize him, and will make your paths straight and smooth [removing obstacles that block your way]."

Day 14 – Boast in the Healing Power of Pure Love

To truly love yourself is under-rated. Loving yourself beyond the less than perfect perceptions of yourself will heal the deepest parts of your soul and spirit. Don't believe the hype of your negative subconscious. I had to funnel through many negative thoughts about myself before I could live a life with confidence; and without low self-esteem.

I learned to love myself and shortly thereafter, my husband was able to find me during this wonderful season! I've always said that marriage is about loving your neighbor as yourself on a deeper level. After funneling through forgiveness, letting go, and mending the broken places in my soul; God allowed me to rebuild with the love that only a husband can give.

My husband loved me so unselfishly that God used it as the last stage of my healing. Ephesians 5:25 represents his love for me.

Ephesians 5:25 AMP says,
25 "Husbands, love your wives [seek the highest good for her and surround her with a caring, unselfish love], just as Christ also loved the church and gave himself up for her,"

<u>**Here's the lesson God gave me for Day 14:**</u>
Love can drive out the negative perceptions about ourselves. Pure love is a healthy, validating power that drives out heartbreak and silences the lies of Satan and the heartbreak of emotional trauma.

Night 14 – Boast in Solving more Problems with Love

My marriage is a testament to a problem that God used my husband to solve in the depths of my soul. My husband loves me how I loved the ex that broke my heart. Because he loves me this way, it's my responsibility to give him what I didn't receive. Although the love expressed in marriage is a powerful source, so it is when we truly learn to love each other. After studying the treasure of the Ephesians 5 marriage while I healed, it reminded me of one of my favorite quotes:

"If lots more of us loved each other, we'd solve lots more problems" – **Louis Armstrong**

Here's the lesson God gave me for Night 14:

Love from friends, family, or spouses has healing properties gained when we love each other in the purest way. Loving each other leads us back to loving ourselves the way Christ commands us to.

Although it's the husband's job to love his wife the way Christ loves the church, it's equally important for us to love one another in a similar and selfless manner.

John 15:12 AMP says,

12 "This is my commandment, that you love and unselfishly seek the best for one another, just as I have loved you."

In vs. 13, you'll see that Jesus also said that there's no one has greater love than to lay down his own life for his friends. Loving others is equally important as loving yourself.

Day **15** – Boast in Childlike Confidence

Rediscover your childlike confidence. Those moments where you believed that you could do anything you put your mind to? Remember? You had no fear, no reservations, and no pre-conceived notion of doubt? When dreaming was second nature; I remember being fearless! Don't stop believing and dreaming! Restoring my belief system was well overdue for my continued confidence in myself, God and others.

Being childlike as an adult may seem difficult. It's easy, but it is uncomfortable for those of us who have put away childish things, so to speak. It's a requirement in view of our relationship with God to be childlike in our confidence, faith, and belief of him. However, it helped me to have this same childlike belief concerning my own belief system.

Childlike -

> …like a child, as in innocence, frankness, etc.; befitting a child: childlike trust

With this definition, the word *frankness* stuck out to me. Children are brutally honest about everything. Instantly I thought, wow! They exemplify what we call *"all or nothing"*.

Here's the lesson God gave me for Day 15:

Being childlike doesn't always mean being sweet and adoring, as we often think of children. It also means being frank in the expression of our beliefs without reservation.

Night 15 – Boast in having Repentant thinking

Figuring out to live as an adult, but think as frankly and as honestly as a child? What a task! It's as simple as opening up ourselves to innocent thinking and believing while operating as an adult. The Holy Spirit, as our comforter, gives us constant reminders to always have a repentant heart daily.

Matthew 18:2-3 AMP says,

2 "He called a little child and set him before them,

3 and said, "I assure you and most solemnly say to you, unless you repent [that is, change your inner self _your old way of thinking, live changed lives] and become like children [trusting, humble, and forgiving], you will never enter the kingdom of heaven."

<u>Here's the lesson God gave me for Night 15:</u>

We should make mature decisions from an innocent point of view about our lives and the world; with the truths that we see through the eyes of a child. Having a repentant way of thinking gives adults the air of innocence needed to always have a childlike belief, faith, and confidence.

As the scripture says, children are trusting, humble, and forgiving. God called to have this same thinking; to maintain the standard of our inner selves and embark on childlike living. Be confident, while being trusting, humble and forgiving. As uncomfortable as this may be, I made it happen for myself. Learning to trust others again through childlike thinking and doing is a principal that keeps our souls free and clear always.

Day 16 – Boast in having Wise counsel

Having the right support is crucial to confidence building. There must be a balance of encouragement and critiques from friends, family, and business associates. Beware! Offense can sometimes cause you to miss out on much-needed advice.

You know that person with their walls up? Afraid to accept critique or advice of any kind because it feels negative? That was me.

Proverbs 15:22-23 AMP says,

22 "Without consultation and wise advice, plans are frustrated, but with many counselors they are established and succeed. 23 A man has joy in giving an appropriate answer, and how good and delightful is a word spoken at the right moment; how good it is!"

Walking daily with the Holy Spirit gives us the confidence we need to discern what's negative and spoken to us in a divine and timely manner. The comforter will never lead you wrong. My mom used to say, "My mind never leads me wrong". Then she would say, "God never leads me wrong!"

<u>Here's the lesson God gave me for Day 16:</u>

Use the Holy Spirit's voice of truth as your filter when accepting critique, advice, and/or counsel from others.

Night **16** – Boast in Drawing the Right Conclusions

No one is devoid of counsel. We all need it to grow properly. We all need it to make the right decisions. Counsel may seem negative, but it's actually an accompaniment to our ability to make the proper conclusions.

Here's the lesson God gave me for Night 16:

Don't draw the wrong conclusions amid counsel. This will steer us off the path of wisdom every time.

Proverbs 12:15-16 AMP says,

15 "The way of the [arrogant] fool [who rejects God's wisdom] is right in his own eyes, but a wise and prudent man is he who listens to counsel.

16 The [arrogant] fool's anger is quickly known [because he lacks self-control and common sense], but a prudent man ignores an insult."

Dear God help us all to be prudent human beings so that we can ignore those insults that don't appear to us as wise counsel! It was the insults of my childhood that I viewed as my life's counsel. Every time the insults instantly replayed in my mind, it caused me to put walls up. I was allowing insults from my past to cloud my judgement of counsel.

My own perpetuated, and created arrogant anger with unforgiveness, caused me to lack self-control; and sometimes common sense.

Day **17** – Boast in Knowing who God IS

There's nothing like a father's, or a mother's words. My dad and mom always knew what to say when I was feeling less than. Family means the world to a child struggling with whom they are. Sometimes in my world, my parents sharing scripture with me just didn't seem to be enough on some days. I learned two things when I analyzed my parents' cheerleading tactics with me. They cheered me on by pointing me back toward scriptural wisdom. However, some days I didn't know how to apply the scriptures to my life. I needed my own personal relationship with God. In learning scriptures, I needed to get an understanding of the God that was represented in them.

<u>**Here's the lesson God gave me for Day 17:**</u>

Seeking the person of God instead of his persona will help you properly apply scripture. In your time of meditation, don't just read because someone else told you to. We must reflect when reading.

I thought that it was my consecration and sanctification alone that helped me apply scripture. Instead, I needed to understand God's relationship with humanity, his character, and to understand how he worked intentionally.

James 1:22 AMP says,

22 "But prove yourselves doers of the word [actively and continually obeying God's precepts], and not merely listeners [who hear the word but fail to internalize its meaning],"

Night **17** – Boast in Understanding his Ways

Have you ever felt like you knew someone? Then you realize that this person is not who you thought they were? It wasn't long before I'd realized that I viewed scripture application the wrong way. My foresight and my hindsight needed to get to know who God was as it pertains to me; not just view him as the God of the bible. He was real. He was God.

Hebrews 5:14 AMP says,
14 "But solid food is for the [spiritually] mature, whose senses are trained by practice to distinguish between what is morally good and what is evil."

It's our job to get to know God. It's also our job to question what's good and evil. These two applied factors forge a healthy relationship. A healthy study life with constant Q&A is the point when getting to know our God.

<u>Here's the lesson God gave me for Night 17:</u>
Don't just study to be better at following the rules of the christian life. Study to get to know who your God is. Learn the how, and the whys of God's personality.

I learned this in hindsight. What a grave lesson that I had to learn. There are thousands, if not millions of people, who suffer from misapplication of scripture. It's like having a road map without understanding how to use it. Reading it and being able to interpret it are two different things. I now have the gift of understanding scripture with perfect insight into life's woes.

Day **18** – Boast in God's Loving Unconditional nature

I thought I knew the power of the blood of Jesus. I thought I understood the sacrifice that he bore for us. I didn't have a clue. The chorus to one of my favorite songs is, "Jesus went to calvary to save a wretch like you and me! That's love". Knowing this alone makes me confident about my life!

I John 4:8-9 AMP says,

8 "The one who does not love has not become acquainted with God [does not and never did know him], for God is love. [He is the originator of love, and it is an enduring attribute of his nature.]

9 By this the love of God was displayed in us, in that God has sent his [one and] only begotten son [the one who is truly unique, the only one of his kind] into the world so that we might live through him."

<u>Here's the lesson God gave me for Day 18:</u>

God's love endures. God's love is in his nature. God's love is unconditional.

There's nothing like the love of God! Even when I don't want his love, he is forever loving me! This same love god has offered to you. There is no love like God's love. If you give him a chance to extend this love to you; its unfailing, eternal presence in life will completely fulfil you.

Night **18** – Boast in God's atoning Sacrifice of Love

We should follow rules made by God; by law, he has to follow the same rules. He needed to fulfil his own requirement to bring the sin of man to justice by giving the ultimate sacrifice of love, his son, to fulfill that requirement. It didn't matter if we loved God or not. He still loved us enough to send his son.

If we keep reading chapter 4 of I John, verse 10, you'll see that he used his own sacrificed son to be a ransom; a sweet, smelling savor. It's only right that I properly interpret the scenario of Jesus' death and use it to feed my own confidence. Knowing that the God I serve will truly choose me every time? This makes me giddy with radiant confidence!

I John 4:10 AMP says,

10 "In this is love, not that we loved God, but that he loved us and sent his son to be the propitiation [that is, the atoning sacrifice, and the satisfying offering] for our sins [fulfilling God's requirement for justice against sin and placating his wrath]."

Here's the lesson God gave me for Night 18:

God's love is unbiased. No matter what we've done, his love still endures to cover us. He will always choose you and I. Our father will do whatever it takes to save us; Yesterday, today, and forever.

Day **19** – Boast in your Amazingness without Envy

We're amazing. God made us to be and do amazing things. Mediocrity can be a trap for many people who can't believe in him or herself enough to pursue beyond the pit of wrong thinking about their capabilities. Declare your amazingness because he made us in his image. God is amazing; So are you. We are all amazing. When we realize how amazing we are, there is no envying. There is no comparison to our neighbor because we understand our differences. You're amazing, even in the eyes of those whom we tend to envy ourselves. What does amazing mean?

Amazing -

...startlingly impressive

Now, let's define *impressive*...

Impressive -

...evoking admiration through size, quality, or skill; grand, imposing, or awesome.

We are surprisingly impressive! Without a doubt, we were already made to give our best impressions; driven by authenticity.

<u>Here's the lesson God gave me for Day 19:</u>

There is no need for envy because we are surprisingly impressive! Without a doubt, we are made to give our best, unique impressions.

Everything about our makeup is all connected. Our mind, body, and soul affect each other. If something is affecting our body, it can affect our minds with anxiety or depression; because our body is in pain, for example. In addition, it may fill the soul of us with emotions of anger because we can't control a certain outcome because of a circumstance or physical sickness.

Proverbs 14:30 AMP says,

30 "A calm and peaceful and tranquil heart is life and health to the body, but passion and envy are like rottenness to the bone."

It matters that we maintain peace and tranquility at all times. It's healthy according to Proverbs 14, verse 30. The same verse says that passion and envy are like rottenness to the bone. Learn to appreciate who you are. There's never a need to envy someone else's body, their life, or their financial status. Envy affects your own personal health. Unhealthy comparison kills.

<u>Here's the lesson God gave me for Night 19:</u>

Never ever envy or compare yourself or your life to someone else. It's unhealthy and unnecessary. Maintain peace at all times. We're amazing. We're impressive. Be at peace.

I wished that I was someone else for many years. Often feeling this way because of other's opinions. Once I found out who I was authentically, I appreciated my own amazing, impressive, authenticity! I am amazing. You are amazing. We are amazing.

Day **20** – Boast in the Power of God's Resurrection

No matter how dead the situation or problem you are facing. He can resurrect the issue! Knowing God in the power of his resurrection is an under-discussed topic; but it's a major appointment to our *confidence* and faith in God. He is the resurrection and the life! He's alive. Tap into the power of his resurrection so you can live!

Sometimes in my life where I felt certain situations were dead. This affected my view of life. Sometimes life's woes can distort our ability to see. We sometimes allow our circumstances to dictate how and what we believe in. The bottom line is this. God can resurrect any situation! The same resurrecting power in Jesus now lives in us.

Philippians 3:10 AMP says,

10 "And this, so that I may know him [experientially, becoming more thoroughly acquainted with him, understanding the remarkable wonders of his person more completely] and [in that same way experience] the power of his resurrection [which overflows and is active in believers], and [that I may share] the fellowship of his sufferings, by being continually conformed [inwardly into his likeness even] to his death [dying as he did];"

Here's the lesson God gave me for Day 20:

Seemingly dead situations and mindsets can be resurrected by the same power that resurrected Jesus. The resurrecting power gives us the upper hand in every area of life. Knowing Jesus in this power helps us to resurrect the dead places in our life.

Every area of our lives can live through the power of his resurrection. What we need in our lives is on the inside of us.

Night 20–Boast in the Resetting power of Resurrection

If I need to wipe my computer clean after a virus, I have to reduce it to a powerless or dead state. I need to reset my PC to start over from a clean slate. When we accept the resurrecting power of Jesus Christ to live on the inside of us; we literally allow God to hit the reset button in our lives. Jesus' death eliminated all of our wrong. This clean slate gives us the hope to start over again.

Ephesians 1:18-19 AMP says,
18 "And [I pray] that the eyes of your heart [the very center and core of your being] may be enlightened [flooded with light by the Holy Spirit], so that you will know and cherish the hope [the divine guarantee, the confident expectation] to which he has called you, the riches of his glorious inheritance in the saints (God's people),
19 and [so that you will begin to know] what the immeasurable and unlimited and surpassing greatness of his [active, spiritual] power is in us who believe. These are in accordance with the working his mighty strength."

<u>Here's the lesson God gave me for Night 20:</u>
Our ability to exist void of sin was reset in Jesus's resurrection. Our ability to start anew in every area of life was reset.

Jesus, during one of his most trying times in the Garden of Gethsemane, allowed death; to reset the lives of the world. He erased the debt of sin in his death. Not just sin, but it gives us a clean slate in every area of life.

Day **21** - Boast knowing you Can Accept compliments

The smallest of compliments can feed the body with the natural endorphins or, (happy juice), that your brain needs to build confidence. Sometimes we replace a healthy compliment with our own criticism about ourselves. Don't be afraid to eat the compliment, chew it, swallow it, & digest it into your esteem's self-conscious.

I was taught very early on that I should say, "Pray for me", when someone gave me a compliment. The church elders of old shared it with me that I needed to be shamefaced to maintain a certain humility as a woman growing up in the culture of the Pentecostal church. This was wise advice. The problem was, I never used the compliments to build a healthy self-esteem. Trying to be humble sometimes left me safeguarded when I truly needed to accept the simplest of compliments.

Proverbs 16:24 AMP says,

24 "Pleasant words are like a honeycomb, sweet and delightful to the soul and healing to the body.

<u>Here's the lesson God gave me for Day 21:</u>

Compliments are a blessing of health to the mind, body, and soul. They feed us with the right neighborly fuel that God intended with his "love thy neighbor" command. They are healthy and needed.

Night **21** - Boast in a Compliment as an Encouragement

I still struggle to look people in the eye; because I used to think it was too arrogant to do so. There was no pep in my step because I didn't think I should own this because of arrogance. I had a blind-sided view of humility while trading against my own self-esteem. With the confusion of arrogance being disguised as confidence, it's hard to know the difference. Fight to know the difference.

Here's the lesson God gave me for Night 21:

We can accept compliments without side effects of arrogant feelings. There's nothing wrong with saying thank you if someone gives you a word of encouragement. Encouraging words are full of life and promotes health in the mind, body, and soul.

Proverbs 15:4 AMP says,

4 "A soothing tongue [speaking words that build up and encourage] is a tree of life, but a perversive tongue [speaking words that overwhelm and depress] crushes the spirit."

If we are taught how to receive encouraging words, we will know how to receive a good word with confidence. Once upon a time, I allowed myself to be overwhelmed and depressed by negative impressions of me. However, I didn't learn, until later, that it was okay to accept compliments as encouragements. There's a thin line between a compliment, a back-handed compliment or an insult. The strange thing is, our bodies will let us know through our own discerning emotions if a comment has crushed our spirit or not.

Day **22** – Boast in your Growing Process

A true diamond grows and goes through several grueling processes before being as beautiful as it's intended to be. Discover your beauty inside. You are a diamond in the rough. You were made to be admired, cared for, and to naturally shine. Sometimes, God wants us to stand the heat in the hottest of kitchens.

Isaiah 48:10-11 AMP says,

10 "Indeed, I have refined you, but not as silver; I have tested and chosen you in the furnace of affliction.

11 For my own sake, for my own sake, I will do it [I refrain and do not completely destroy you]; For how can my name be defiled and profaned [as it would if my chosen people were completely destroyed]?"

<u>Here's the lesson God gave me for Day 22:</u>

God treats us in a certain way to make sure we are properly growing. He takes us through fiery trials that come to try our faith.

Afflictions, circumstances, trials come to build us up; never to destroy us. It takes different solvents to pre-clean and clean a diamond. It's exposed to extremely high heat during the refining process. In order for us to shine, we must go through the refiner's fire. As soon as we go through the process and show signs of growth, then God will put us on display. You may feel that you're in a season of hiding. God has plans to put you on display. Your light will shine brighter than you'll ever know!

Night **22** – Boast in God's Deliverance

It doesn't matter what God seems to test us with. Whether it's sickness, broken relationships, or financial distress; He will deliver us out of every circumstance. During the process, we may seem helpless because of the noise surrounding our minds. Going through will attack our confidence, our self-esteem, and our ability to think straight.

Psalm 34:19 AMP says,

19 "Many hardships and perplexing circumstances confront the righteous, but the Lord rescues him from them all."

Here's the lesson God gave me for Day 22:

When we are afflicted, it gives God an opportunity to fix things for us. He wants to get all the glory when things are going well and when things are not so well. He'll deliver you if you let him.

1 Peter 4:12-13 AMP says,

12 "Beloved, do not be surprised at the fiery ordeal which is taking place to test you [that is, to test the quality of your faith], as though something strange or unusual were happening to you.
13 But insofar as you are sharing Christ's sufferings, keep on rejoicing, so that when his glory [filled with his radiance and splendor] is revealed, you may rejoice with great joy."

Just as diamonds are put on display, God will do the same for us after we've shown a significant amount of growth. The point is to get through so that we can help someone else.

Day *23* – Boast in Risking "IT" to Build Confidence

Taking risks and chances starts when we're young. Small confidence lessons for children will invest in a more confident adulthood in their future. There's nothing like learning the importance of confident risk taking at an early age. Unfortunately, I began doubting myself as a child. I didn't recover from this until years later. In my life, I've learned that taking chances with the right God-centered perspectives proved beneficial; especially to my confidence. Taking a chance propelled my confidence even further. Whatever your it is, don't be afraid. Always believe that God has your life under his control. If he said it, you can believe it.

Risk -

...to venture upon; take or run the chance of

Being able to take chances depends on our ability to give the control of our entire life to God. We should trust him to answer when we call or ask him questions about our purpose; This will sear a soulful confidence to live a life of strength.

Psalm 138:3 AMP says,

3 "On the day I called, you answered me; And you made me bold and confident with [renewed] strength in my life"

Here's the lesson God gave me for Day 23:

Knowing that God will never leave us or forsake us, gives a bold sense of confidence for risk taking.

Night 23 – Boast in Being Bold and Content

Be bold! He is always there! No matter what it looks like, know that God will never leave you nor forsake you. Always have a posture to pass the test while being content. Even his silence will shock you into an unwavering confidence. God is always watching how we handle certain things. He wants to know that our character can be flawless even when our circumstances may not be. While we the world that seems to be glued to the love of money, success with God is key. We can be bold in our God-given visions, while being grateful and content. Besides, it's our inner growth that counts.

Hebrews 13:5 AMP says,

5 "Let your character [your moral essence, your inner nature] be free from the love of money [shun greed-be financially ethical], being content with what you have; for he has said, "I will never [under any circumstances] desert you [nor give you up nor leave you without support, nor will I in any degree leave you helpless], nor will I forsake or let you down or relax my hold on you [assuredly not]!"

<u>Here's the lesson God gave me for Night 23:</u>

Being content is just as important as being bold when taking chances. Practice gratefulness to solidify contentment. Take chances to show God and others that you are relentlessly bold in trusting your life's purpose to his will. He won't leave you, nor forsake you.

Day **24** – Boast in Not Giving Up

Regardless of the hell you've gone through, believe only what God has promised! Don't stop! You will get to your destination! You can't give up. You can't throw in the towel. Put down your white flag! There is a prize to be won if you finish a confident race. I learned that I had a unique pace to my destination. Don't let comparison kill or waste your time.

Remember the story about the race between the Tortoise and the Hare that we learned as children? Comparison deceived the rabbit. This caused him to give up before it was time. The hare was faster, but the tortoise had an understanding; he kept moving. He finished the race. How fast or slow? It doesn't matter. God gives each of us a space of time that should be focused for a good faith fight. Don't give up.

Ecclesiastes 9:10-11 KJV says,

10 Whatsoever thy hand findeth to do, do it with thy might; for there is no work, nor device, nor knowledge, nor wisdom, in the grave, whither thou goest.

11 I returned, and saw under the sun, that the race is not to the swift, nor the battle to the strong, neither yet bread to the wise, nor yet riches to men of understanding, nor yet favour to men of skill; but time and chance happeneth to them all.

<u>**Here's the lesson God gave me for Day 24:**</u>

When you understand the reason for the journey, the destination won't really matter. Focusing on the present will always keep you steady in life's race; no matter how fast or how slow you are going.

Night 24 – Boast in Your Own Lane

The tortoise was confident at his own unique pace. He didn't give up. He kept going. He kept looking forward. He never looked back. He didn't look to the right. He didn't look to the left. He kept putting one foot in front of the other.

2 Timothy 4:7 KJV says,
7 "I have fought a good fight, I have finished my course, I have kept the faith:"

Paul tells Timothy that he finished his course. Every journey is unique to the runner. You have your own course or race to focus on; no one else's. Don't be like the hare who, in noticing his opponent's weaknesses, over-estimated himself; and under-estimated his neighbor.

<u>Here's the lesson God gave me for Night 24:</u>
Don't be like the hare who showed his brawn instead of his mental endurance. When you're focused on mental endurance, you'll be focused on keeping your own lane free of distractions. You won't even have time to flex for other people. You'll safely get to your destination.

Your lane is not up for comparison. Your purpose is not up for comparison. God never meant you for you to compare to your neighbor. Because we are all unique as God's creation, he never intended for us to compare; but to complement each other.

Day **25** – Boast in God's Strength if your Heart Fails

So, you say you're a failure? You've fallen? In our moments of fleshly weakness and failure, God is our inheritance of mercy that will always be available to all who ask. God says he would be our portion forever! He says we can get up from the fallen areas of life.

There is a song I love by Stephen Hurd called "Lead me to the Rock". It says, "when my heart is overwhelmed, lead me to the rock that is higher than I." Just as the song says, when I'm overwhelmed in my own flesh and weakness, I can lean on God's strength. It will take me through the rest of the way.

Psalm 73:26 5:16 AMP says,
26 My flesh and my heart may fail, But God is the rock and strength of my heart and my portion forever.

He is my portion. He is my possession. He is my legacy. He is my reward. He is my award. He is my flattery. He is my partaker. He is my rock. He is my refuge. He is my fortress. He is the quencher of my thirst. He is my courage. He is my *God!* He takes complete joy when we totally lean and trust in him.

<u>**Here's the lesson God gave me for Day 25:**</u>
You are not a failure. When your heart and flesh fail you, God will always be the rock that you can lean on. His strength is always waiting to lift us in our weak moments. A failure is a learning opportunity. Learn the lesson and keep going.

Night **25** – Boast in your Strength being made Perfect

Every time we present unto God our flesh and its weaknesses, we accept his grace. We win against our flesh with the grace of God.

2 Corinthians 12:9 AMP says,

9 but He has said to me, "My grace is sufficient for you [My lovingkindness and My mercy are more than enough— always available—regardless of the situation]; for [My] power is being perfected [and is completed and shows itself most effectively] in [your] weakness." Therefore, I will all the more gladly boast in my weaknesses, so that the power of Christ [may completely enfold me and] may dwell in me."

If you can understand the Daddy-daughter concept? You can understand this scripture. When a daughter runs to her daddy to tell him her problem, she expects his strength to go to bat for her in her weakest moments. So, it is with God! His strength is made perfect in our weakness. His strength is made perfect when we trust our daddy God with our weaknesses.

Here's the lesson God gave me for Night 25:

We are expected to be strong at all times. However, we are expected to accept his sufficient grace to combat all of our weaknesses. God delights in our weakest moments because he will glory in coming to our aid with the weapon of grace. Got a problem? Go tell your daddy. He'll grace you to be strong in every obstacle.

Day **26** – Boast in Being Present Intentionally

Don't allow the guilt of your past or the anxiety caused by thoughts of what lies in your future, to keep you from living in your present. Learn how to take it one day at a time. Being better takes time. But we must nurture your today with faith and belief to count. Love the *today* you've been given! Your *today* needs a sober-minded you to take it one day at a time!

I found that in my personal progress, taking one day at a time helped in *rebuilding* my confidence. Learning how to be *present* in the moment was seemingly new to me. I not only had to take it one day at a time; I took it one minute at a time. I needed to rebuild my way of thinking *daily*.

2 Corinthians 4:16 AMP says,
16 Therefore we do not become discouraged [spiritless, disappointed, or afraid]. Though our outer self is [progressively] wasting away, yet our inner self is being [progressively] renewed day by day.

Time is more precious than any priceless resource known to humanity. I had to learn how to use my own time wisely by intentionally being present every single day.

Here's the lesson God gave me for Day 26:

Reflect on your past without dwelling on it and emotionally staying there. Plan for the future, without obsessing over it. Live in your present as if it will be your last time on earth.

Night **26** – Boast in a Renewed Mind

The bible declares that we should renew our mind daily. This allows us to focus on the issues of today rather than the faux pas of yesterday or the snafus of tomorrow. Everything consequently happens for a reason.

Romans 12:2 AMP says,

*2"And do not be conformed to this world [any longer with its superficial values and customs], but be transformed and progressively changed [as you mature spiritually] by the **renewing of your mind** [focusing on godly values and ethical attitudes], so that you may prove [for **your**selves] what the will **of** God is, that which is good and acceptable and perfect [in His plan and purpose for you]".*

When we allow the world to dictate our focus, we unintentionally become immature in our thinking and our view of life. Being confident in the will of God for your lives requires you and I to stay mindful of keeping godly values and attitudes.

<u>**Here's the lesson God gave me for Night 26:**</u>
Don't regret your past or worrying about your future. Depression or anxiety doesn't have to be your life's present posture. Be mature. Be transformed. Be thoughtful. Be renewed.

Renew -

...to make like new: restore to freshness, vigor or perfection.

Day **27** – Boast with Godly Focus; Be God-Focused

You can succeed if you stay focused. Focus is hard but is worth the fruits of your labor. Every task that was ever completed, whether mental, or physical, breeds feelings of accomplishment. Accomplishment produces an even healthier outlook; this embeds your conscience with more confidence.

Proverbs 4:25-26 AMP says,

25 "Let your eyes look directly ahead [toward the path of moral courage] And let your gaze be fixed straight in front of you [toward the path of integrity].
26 Consider well and watch carefully the path of your feet, and all your ways will be steadfast and sure."

The only way to have godly focus, is to keep looking and moving forward. Don't miss out on opportunities for a lack of concentration. Before intentionally healing, I was really horrible about concentrating on most things. My self-pity always caused me to give up on most ventures. I ultimately accepted it.

Focus -

…pay particular attention to.

<u>Here's the lesson God gave me for Day 27:</u>
To focus, you need to have something to focus on. Knowing and understanding your God-given purpose will direct your daily focus.

Night 27 – Boast in Your own Confident Integrity

Integrity is one of life's greatest guides. We talk about it quite a bit. Many don't always understand how important integrity is to an intentionally good confident character. Sometimes the word itself gets lost in translation with people of faith. My integrity was something that I'd always held dear. Defining integrity in my life was a bit shaky concerning my confident moments. Sometimes my integral moments boasted an overkill of *kindness for blindness*; so-to speak? I was able to rebuild it by defining it according to who God called me to be.

Integrity -
...an undivided or unbroken completeness or totality with nothing wanting.

Down through the years, I constantly shared fairness and integrity with everyone else; except myself.

Proverbs 11:3 AMP says,
3 "The integrity and moral courage of the upright will guide them, But the crookedness of the treacherous will destroy them."

<u>Here's the lesson God gave me for Night 27:</u>
Maintain your integrity despite the works of others. Integrity is not only a guide for you to treat others fairly. It's also a guide for you to treat yourself fairly. Be whole in your own integrity.

Day **28** – Boast in the Power of Your Smile

Find something to *smile* about today! A simple, but genuine *smile* can take you through your day. Smiling is therapeutic and helps not only you; but also, those around you. A *smile* is contagious! I made a practice of finding something to smile about daily. As I'm writing this wonderful chapter, I'm reminded to add a smile to my devoted journey. I remind myself to smile *gratefully* every single day. No matter what or whom I come in contact with, I've learned to just *smile.* .

Job 29:24 AMP says,

24 " I smiled at them when they did not believe, and they did not diminish the light of my face."

Please take some time to get acquainted with Job's story. It's extraordinary! He experienced so much loss and disappointment; yet he was able to smile in the face of the disbelief of his friends. Never let others diminish the power of your smile.

<u>Here's the lesson God gave me for Day 28:</u>

A smile is a powerful thing. It can be a weapon; used for good. Use it to heal yourself in moments of gratefulness. Use it to heal others in moments of disbelief. Keep smiling.

Even when it's hard to do so, there's will always be something to *smile* about.

Night 28 – Boast in Gratitude's Influence

When others see you going through with a smile of gratitude, it influences their outlook on life. Someone is always watching and looking up to you. There's always that one person who lives on your every word; whether you believe it. We are all secretly and unknowingly mentoring someone. The reward of constant gratitude is the ability to influence someone else along the way. Isn't that a true blessing?

Psalm 145:6 AMP says,

6 " People will speak of the power of your awesome acts, and [with gratitude and submissive wonder] I will tell of your greatness."

We rarely spread our gratitude as the old saints of the Bible did in yesteryear. Unfortunately, in some ways, we've reduced our gratitude to a social media post, or a light hug with a church member; while sharing with them how the week went.

<u>**Here's the lesson God gave me for Night 28:**</u>

Gratitude has an overwhelming effect on the person influenced by its presence. Don't be afraid to show gratitude. Don't just share gratitude lightly. Share it intentionally to others who could be influenced by the root of your gratitude of God and having life.

Be infectious while sharing your day-to-day successes with your neighbor. Someone needs to see you being grateful at every turn. Someone needs to see you naturally being grateful even in your least grateful moments. *Be* and live *gratefully.*

Day 29 – Boast in Creating Good Habits

If your struggling in an area, devote a full thirty minutes a day to not only bettering yourself, but change your thought process. Do this thing for 60 days. It will start you down a much more confident path through repetition and recreating a different thought pattern consciously every day. Jesus's habits were a great road map for me to learn from.

Here's the lesson God gave me for Day 29:

A practice of good habits will promote confidence daily. But practicing a habit that reflects who you are is even better.

Good habit forming is key. Preparation is huge a breeder of confidence. God said to me that I wasn't spending enough time practicing the core of who I was as a person. I was practicing quite a bit without the essence of me.

Habit -

…a settled or regular tendency or practice, especially one that is hard to give up.

I discussed in Day 1 how important it was to being your authentic self. I did many things to please others. Now, I make it a point to practice the authenticity of my empathetic nature in every habit. This is the only way for me to own good habits. I followed God's example after I knew who I was destined to be.

Ephesians 5:1 AMP says,

1 " Therefore be imitators of God, as beloved children."

Night **29** – Boast in Daily Declarations

What exactly is a declaration? How are we supposed to use them? I only knew of this word because I'd been in church all my life. I'd hear preachers say it over us. Ministers, for example, would say, "I decree and declare that you are healed in Jesus name!" I thought I knew how to define the word *declare*. I was pleasantly surprised to know what it truly meant.

Let's define the word *declare*:

Declare -

> 1. say something in a solemn and emphatic matter;
> 2. reveal one's intentions or identity;
> 3. express feelings of love to someone.

Learning to declare over myself each day, in the proper manner? This new habit had to do with God and my personal beliefs alone. I needed to believe. One of my favorite scriptures uses this word. Declaring is about the feeling that comes with it. When I read or declare this scripture, I feel it. I believe it. To declare? You must *feel* it. You must *believe* it. I began to practice and expressed declarations that felt just like it does when I read this scripture.

Psalm 118:17 AMP says,

17 "I will not die, but live, and declare the works and recount the illustrious acts of the Lord."

<u>**Here's the lesson God gave me for Night 29:**</u>

You can't declare without belief effectively. Declare it. Believe it.

Day **30** – Boast in Pure Joy

Joy is inevitable when we are doing those things that we desire to do. Think about the last time you were genuinely joyful. What happened? Questioning how your joy left can very well lead to a solution to your lack of Joy. True freedom is in a desire. Joy begets *confidence.* Go get your joy! It really didn't go that far. Look inside yourself. A wise person once said that joy was an internal gift, but happiness is an external gift. Joy is enabled from the inside; happiness depends on external circumstance.

Joy -

> ...the emotion evoked by well-being and doing what one desires

Joy comes when we involve something that we want to do! Take inventory of your life. Are you doing something that you truly want to do? If not, what are you waiting for? My soul's joy depended on time spent with God. Getting to know myself while getting to know him? It's a beautiful process! I'm still getting to know the both of us!

Here's the lesson God gave me for Day 30:

The more you stay in God's presence, the more you will desire the things of God. Your joy will be full and complete.

Psalm 16:11 AMP says,

11 "You will show me the path of life; In your presence is fullness of joy; In your right hand there are pleasures forevermore."

Night **30** – Boast in having Godly Desires

If it were up to me, I would never have been a preacher. As a teenager trying to get to know God, ministering was the furthest thing from my mind. I remember wanting to be a singer. I wanted to be a teacher. I also wanted to be a computer programmer. I even wanted to be a poet! As my desires changed in my twenties, I delighted myself in the desires of God! I wanted what God wanted for me. The more I delighted in God, the more my own desires became less valid.

Psalm 34:7 AMP says,

17 "Delight yourself in the Lord, and he will give you the desires and petitions of your heart."

Delight -

...take pleasure in; to please

There were things that I wanted. After allowing God to help guide my life, those wants changed. In the middle of me wanting more of God, he gave me the desires of my heart. However, my heart's desires changed to Godly desires.

Here's the lesson God gave me for Night 30:

No one knows you better than your creator. Your relationship with God influences your desires. Delighting yourself in him is the first step to gaining Godly desires.

I want what God wants for me. You should want what God wants for you. We all should want what God wants for us all.

Day 31 – Boast in Healthy Motives

My day 31 definitely has an overflow of day 30. The thing about delighting yourself in the Lord; it ensures the right motives. Building confidence takes right intentions and healthy motives. Be confident, never forgetting your true motive or reason for doing a thing. Ensuring that I kept my desires in line with God's heartbeat or purpose for my life secures and protects healthy motives within myself.

Proverbs 16:2 AMP says,

2 *"All the ways of a man are clean and innocent in his own eyes [and he may see nothing wrong with his actions], But the Lord weighs and examines the motives and intents [of the heart and knows the truth].*

Here's the lesson God gave me for Day 31:

God has given us a wonderful map in scripture to guide our motives and intents. Don't assume that your ways carry the right intent. Allow God to give you guidance.

The part that I don't want you to miss is the word *healthy.* We all have motives. They just have to be healthy.

Healthy -

...the state of being free from illness or injury.

Your motives should have no ill-will behind them. Only a healthy relationship with God can ensure healthy motives.

Night 31 – Boast in Rewarding Yourself

More important to confidence is reward and constant evaluation of completed tasks and goals. Reward your efforts and completion. I can honestly say that this is something that I've never done. Rewarding myself? Even the thought of doing this seems unnatural.

This is what I found in my personal walk. Allowing God into my life and trusting him with his plan causes me to succeed. I realized that it was ok to reward myself as an encouraging mechanism to build confidence. Knowing and trusting God is a great reason to reward me when things are going right.

Proverbs 16:3 AMP says,

3 Commit your works to the Lord [submit and trust them to him], And your plans will succeed [if you respond to His will and guidance]."

<u>**Here's the lesson God gave me for Night 31:**</u>

We should celebrate success. Success inside of God's plan should be rewarded. However, it's your job to respond to his will and accept his guidance. Your reward will be inevitable.

Reward -

...receive what one deserves in recognition of efforts or achievements.

Day *32* – Boast in the Root of your Excitement

Find your excitement. I believe that a spirit-filled, God-influenced life was not that exciting. This very thought also affected my own self-esteem in my teenage years because of my upbringing. However, it is exciting when you can find the point of your individual excitement.

We all have this excitement or potential muse. Spiritually, mentally and soulfully, there are things that make us excited to exist in this world. Finding out what excites or stimulates you is simple. As I studied the notion of my own excitement, I realized what God's excitement was!

You and I are God's excitement! Our very existence thrills him. We are his thrilling creation. The zeal and zest of his being! His fevering love for us causes his titillating excitement. He desires for us to feel the same for him.

Psalm 34:9 AMP says,

8 "O taste and see that the Lord [our God] is good; How blessed [fortunate, prosperous, and favored by God] is the man who takes refuge in him."

Here's the lesson God gave me for Day 32:

God wants the love for him to be a mechanism for excitement as we are his. Experiencing his fire should excite us.

Night *32* – Boast in your spiritual Fire

After going over the day's notes about excitement, I realized how similar this word was to another word; fire. When excitement points properly within my relationship with God, I can find my passion or my fire.

We all have a certain individual fire that makes us all unique. It's that fire that helps us feel alive. I discussed earlier about my super power of empathy. The more I use my unique, empathetic personality, the more passionate I am about gaining opportunities to express it!

Fire -
…fervent or passionate emotion or enthusiasm.

Here's the lesson God gave me for Night 32:

Find your Fire; that thing that constantly keeps you awake at night. Find your unique passion. There is a fire waiting inside of God's will for your life. This fire is the thing that will keep you going.

It was the pain that gave me my passion. Listening was my fire. I found that listening gave me a reward of fulfillment while helping others. There is something to that burning desire that God just won't let you shake. This is how it was for me when I listened intently to someone in pain. I wanted to help people heal in the same areas that I failed in for so many years. My excitement. My fire. My enthusiasm. My eagerness. My own zeal and zest for life kept my spiritual fire burning. Your fire is unchanging; it is unique to *you*.

Day *33* – Boast in Surrendering to God

I found that confidence was second nature to me when I surrendered to God. Not day by day, but minute by minute. Constantly changing your will to what God wants is simply the act of surrendering. Don't take one minute for granite. Being in church all my life, I assumed that I was surrendering. However, the surrender happened during my alone time.

There was a time in my life where my spiritual community time trumped my alone time with God. That was the difference. Spending time at church is about staying connected with the people of God. Spending time alone with God is about your individual relationship. When you don't have the proper balance of time with God and his people, you will be busy being busy without the proper spiritual freedom or direction.

<u>Here's the lesson God gave me for Day 33:</u>

In all of your serving, don't forget to surrender to the God that you're serving.

Job 11:13 CEV says,

13 "Surrender your heart to God, turn to him in prayer."

There are many confident Christians running around without accepting the sweet invitation of surrendering to God! Churching and serving is one thing; but actively having a daily dialogue with God is another. Let God be there for you by surrendering to his love for you. Turn to him in prayer.

Night *33* – Boast in Knowing who your Enemy Is

I think that when we don't properly surrender all to God, we position him in our lives as our enemy without realizing it. When we try to control so much of our lives, we don't recognize the omission of the creator.

We assume that God is the enemy sometimes because of what he allows us to go through. His intent is never to be our enemy. His intent is to draw you closer to him. God is on our side. He is on our team. God isn't the enemy. In this game called life, he is our coach.

Surrender -

…cease resistance to an enemy or opponent and submit to their authority.

<u>Here's the lesson God gave me for Night 33:</u>

God isn't your opponent. Satan is. God isn't your enemy. Satan is.

Never resist the one who created you. We seem to only believe what we can see and feel. I can honestly say that the more I draw closer to God, the more I feel in tuned with how much he cares about me. We have to surrender whole heartedly without resistance.

James 4:7 AMP says,

7 "So submit to [the authority of] God. Resist the devil [stand firm against him] and he will flee from you."

Day **34** – Boast in being More than a Conqueror

We are more than conquerors. We are more than survivors. As you can see, the closer I got to the end of my 40 days; the more God had me to research and define my day-to-day concepts. I'd heard the scripture about being more than a conqueror during my entire childhood. It was time now to get more acquainted with this scripture as an adult.

Romans 8:37 AMP says,

37 "Yet in all these things we are more than conquerors and gain an overwhelming victory through Him who loved us [so much that He died for us]."

Not only have we been able to subdue Satan, our victory over him is a definite for us eternally; but also internally. We get to not only master Satan forever, but we get to master ourselves. We are more than conquerors because we have a surpassing victory through Christ Jesus. Because of Jesus' testimony; because of his life as he lived it, we are overcomers.

<u>Here's the lesson God gave me for Day 34:</u>

A conqueror wins, but the overcomer uses the win and the enemy in pursuit of the greater picture of his or her purpose. The overcomer puts every circumstance into perspective.

Don't just survive, dear friends. Don't just conquer. Be an overcomer. In the end, your life will testify on your behalf as an overcomer; not as a survivor or even as a conqueror.

Night **34** – Boast in being an Overcomer

I was asking God why he didn't just want me to survive. The Holy Spirit said to me that surviving gives the notion that danger is still lurking around. He said that the overcomer knows that he is covered by the blood, assuming success. The survivor sometimes takes the glory for their own survival. However, the overcomer appreciates the person, thing, or circumstance that caused them to overcome. The difference is, the overcomer is never alone! Jesus caused us to be overcomers. We couldn't survive the victory of the cross on our own. It was the covering of Christ that caused us to overcome!

Survive -

…continue to live or exist, especially in spite of danger or hardship.

Overcome -

…succeed in dealing with a problem or difficulty, or opponent; prevail or get control.

Here's the lesson God gave me for Night 34:

Don't just be victorious, despite the devil's antics. Be victorious because you've prevailed successfully with God's help. Don't just exist to survive. Live daily to succeed by overcoming daily.

Don't just survive despite your adversity. Defeat it! We are winners. We can be successful *overcomers* in Christ! We are not here just to conquer and survive! God calls us to surpassing greatness and victories! We are *Overcomers!*

Day **35** – Boast in being Open to New Experiences

What we see inspires us. To become more, become exposed to more. The more we see, the more our strength to become releases. When you have never been exposed to anything, you can become very critical, and narrowminded, and very judgmental. You'll see the world through the lens of your experiences. You'll close doors on yourself that God was trying to open for you.

My pain drove me away from my hometown. It literally forced me to gain new experiences. Although I gained wonderful new experiences, I viewed my experiences through a limited lens. This lens was based on my hometown. My view of the world was a *fish bowl* view. I desperately needed to fix this.

Isaiah 43:18-19 AMP says,

18 "Do not remember the former things, or ponder the things of the past.

19 Listen carefully, I am about to do a new thing, now it will spring forth; Will you not be aware of it? I will even put a road in the wilderness, Rivers in the desert."

<u>Here's the lesson God gave me for Day 35:</u>

Stay open to change. Always challenge what you think you know by gaining new experiences. Don't let your past keep you stagnant.

Experiences are like immortal meals that will stick to your bones for a lifetime. These experiences give wisdom from the bad moments and healthy memories from the good moments.

93

Night **35** – Boast in Exposing yourself to New people

I am that person who cowers to the wall to just hang there. I'm probably the quietest wall flower that you will ever meet. I was extremely introverted because of my childhood. The era of my twenties brought on more introverted tendencies because of hurt from others in certain relationships and friendships. A certain timeline of events caused me to no longer allow others to get close to me.

A part of my healing process meant dealing with my inability to connect with new people. Now that I'd walked through healing, through forgiveness, I was ready to expose myself again to others.

Matthew 5:43-44 AMP says,

43 "You have heard that it was said, 'You shall love your neighbor (fellow man) and hate your enemy.
44 But I say to you, love [that is, unselfishly seek the best higher good for] your enemies and pray for those who persecute you,"

<u>Here's the lesson God gave me for Night 35</u>:

Heal your past quirks about people. Don't be unwilling to connect with new people. God uses people to be a blessing to other people. Don't cutoff the blessing that comes with relationship with your neighbor.

With everything that we indulge in, there has to be a balance. Too much exposure to the sun can hurt us. Not enough exposure to the sun can cause us to miss out on nature's vitamins. Experience people with the leading of the Holy spirit.

Day **36** – Boast in Being Fearless

Do not be afraid. Fear causing obstacles don't have to be boulders in our path. They can be scary, but they are always stepping stones to a higher purpose. Hold yourself up to the light of who God intends for you to be; look at the steps he's carved into the rocks of life before you. Uncover your buried treasure chest of talents and abilities and risk them serving God. Always persevere toward the vision of what you were made for; without fear.

My purpose is carved into the rocks of life for me; through every obstacle that I'd ever gone through. The word vision is important. Honestly? This word never has held as much meaning as it does to my life as it does now! God had always given me a vision. I couldn't always execute them because I was afraid. I'm no longer a slave to fear!

<u>Here's the lesson God gave me for Day 36:</u>

Realize God's presence. Fear cannot stay when we know that God is present with us.

Psalm 118:6a NIV says,

6 "The Lord is with me; I will not be afraid."

I've learned to speak to God in my moments of fear. When he says to me, *"Felicia, I'm with you."*, it makes all the difference in the world! There is nothing like sweet nothings being whispered in your ear by the Holy Spirit.

Night **36** – Boast in God's Peace

There's a calmness to God's voice that takes all of my anxiety and worry away! When God's peace overshadows you, you can be confident without knowing the outcome of your current circumstance. His peace will overwhelm; pressing upon you a calming demeanor.

John 14:27 AMP says,

27 "Peace I leave with you; My [perfect] peace I give to you; not as the world gives, do I give to you. Do not let your heart be troubled, nor let it be afraid. [Let my perfect peace calm you in every circumstance and give you courage and strength for every challenge.]"

<u>Here's the lesson God gave me for Night 36:</u>

God's peace is no match for your fear and anxiety. Giving us peace is his good pleasure. Everything that God has for us has to always be accepted. We must accept his peace in our daily lives.

Adulting can be hard sometimes. Unfortunately, as adults, we tend to not express ourselves in our moments of disquiet and agony. We tend to just keep it moving. Sometimes this is not healthy. Sometimes keeping it moving, at least for me, kept the peace of God away from me. It's ok to keep it moving. However, it's also ok to stop to process and reach for peace. When we accept the peace of God, we gain courage and strength needed to meet every challenge; just as scripture says.

Day **37** – Boast in your Support system

Who is in your village? You know, the people that hold you accountable to having healthy confidence? Be sure that your friends and family are genuinely supporting you. It was more important than I ever realized in my own personal life.

I wanted the confidence that some of my family and friends displayed. Unfortunately, my friends/family alike could never usher me into a conversation about having more confidence while I was in the comfort zone of low self-esteem. They'd never brought it up, really; it was a sore thumb for me. This is my former regret; now my reflection. I am now always assured that the people who support me are holding me accountable in my thinking. Having people in my corner that will help me stay on this path of confidence, not just spectate while I waddle in self-pity, is of the utmost importance.

Psalm 54:4 AMPC says,

4 "Behold, God is my helper and ally; the Lord is my upholder and is with them who uphold my life."

<u>Here's the lesson God gave me for Day 37:</u>

Uphold in this sense means to support or sustain; someone that upholds you, let's you lean on them. Connect with people who help uphold your life in this manner.

Uphold is a verb. No action? No support. It's a word that requires action. Anyone in your circle should support you while they're in your presence; but also while out of your presence.

Night **37** – Boast in Becoming a Better Friend

Evaluating my friendships and my circle was key to my healing. However, this reflective state caused me to evaluate myself as a friend. I desperately wanted to be better with not only my friends, but with just being friendly. I asked myself a series of questions with the help of the Holy Spirit, according to a verse I sought in Ecclesiastes.

Ecclesiastes 4:10 AMP says,
10 For if they fall, the one will lift up his fellow. But woe to him who is alone when he falls and has not another to lift him up!"

This scripture caused me to examine myself by asking; do I have people that I can be there for if they fall. It pleased me that my spirit gave a resounding yes! However, I didn't feel that others would do this for me. In looking at my circle, I attempted to be sure that I was a better friend, a better wife, a better daughter, and a better sister. It didn't matter that I questioned others motives as my friend. It only mattered that I wanted to be a better friend. I realized I was an enabler. Those I helped emotionally weren't equip to give me the same measure of help. I didn't allow them to be there for me this way. Go figure!

<u>Here's the lesson God gave me for Night 37:</u>
You will always reap what you've sown. If you uplift one, another will uplift you. Just be a better friend through evaluation of your own fruit from your past or current friendships.

Day 38 – Boast in being Honest with God

God is the best listener. Don't be afraid to talk to God. He loves dialogue with you. Yes, he will talk back to you! God and I have had the realist conversations. Even in sharing these conversations with you, please know that it warms my heart to share the person of God as a comforter and a great listener! You can literally pray or talk to him anywhere about anything!

I carried around so much unforgiveness that I almost gave up my right to carry the gospel of truth in a manner that pleased God. Like David, my foot had slipped! My confidence was more about having a godly posture rather than putting the self-loathing tendencies in check that I'd harbored. I needed to find the balance, just like David did in Psalm 94.

Psalm 94:17-18 AMP says,
17"If the Lord had not been my help, I would soon have dwelt in [the land of silence.
18 If I say, "My foot has slipped," Your compassion and lovingkindness, O Lord, will hold me up.

If it had not been for the Lord on my side; where would I be! God will always be there to guide you and I from pitfalls.

<u>**Here's the lesson God gave me for Day 38:**</u>
His compassion and lovingkindness will always be there to hold you up. There is no reason to be so afraid of God that you can't be honest with him!

Night 38 -Boast in Forgiving God

I found that the more I forgave, the more I allowed the compassion and lovingkindness of God to come into my heart. Forgiving held me up. I opened my eyes to knowing that this same standard of godly justice, godly compassion & godly love that I discussed in Night 1? It was always there to help me hold myself accountable. I needed to finally realize who held the right to vengeance. Vengeance was God's alone. It was not my job. However, learning to react in a godly manner took going deeper in my relationship with God. As close as I thought I was to the Lord, I needed to get even closer to him for my own personal intervention to *forgive* a *blameless* God. Wait, what!

I kept going boldly before the throne of grace so I could finally become a student of grace! I found that going bold didn't mean yelling and screaming at God because of what I went through. There was a simple formula that God required of me in my individual healing. It was honesty. I found that coming boldly to the throne of grace meant that I could truly share any and every emotion with God, my abba father. The more I came to him as a child versus a leadership servant, I could truly cast all of my cares on him. Not just some of them, but all of them. I had to make a serious decision during my own self-discovery to confront feelings of resentment towards God. In my own self-discovery, I asked myself; Do I need to entertain the notion of forgiving God? Forgive God? Not that God even needed my forgiveness, but he needed me to confront those feelings of unforgiveness towards him. Blaming God is something that we don't want to discuss. Although we shouldn't blame God, it's a natural reaction when we don't understand why he allows certain things to happen; in those moments that we feel he could intervene. I had to admit that I held resentment towards God.

Forgive -
…stop feeling angry or resentful toward someone.

I realized forgiving God isn't such a horrible or disrespectful notion. I didn't have to be afraid to admit that I was angry and resentful towards my creator for allowing me to go through certain things.

Here's the lesson God gave me for Night 38:

It's ok to admit resentment towards God. Before you blame God, gain clarity about your situation. Don't waste your time resenting God. There's a purpose for everything that we go through.

Psalm 18:30-33 AMP says,

30 "As for God, His way is blameless. The word of the Lord is tested [it is perfect, it is faultless]; He is a shield to all who take refuge in Him.

31 For who is God, but the Lord? Or who is a rock except our God,

32 The God who encircles me with strength and makes my way blameless?

33 He sets my feet like hinds' feet [able to stand firmly and tread safely on paths of testing and trouble]; He sets me [securely] upon my high places.

I needed to stop blaming God, just like I needed to stop blaming people. I forgave God and people! He is blameless!

Day **39** – Boast in having Strong Faith

Don't let your struggles fool you. Your faith is still strong. Began working your faith in your more confident areas. This way, confidence will sustain; and will automatically encourage you along the way through your less confident areas.

Faith -

...complete trust or confidence in someone or something.

It was important for me to listen intently to the wisdom of the Holy Spirit, to evaluate whether my faith was strong. I needed to explore two things. I'd always wandered about the differences between *having faith* and *believing*.

Believe -

...accept (something) as true; feel sure of the truth of.

<u>Here's the lesson God gave me for Day 39:</u>

Confidence and trust are complete when your hope includes the act of believing. You mustn't have just trust and confidence. You must accept it as truth before your desired miracle manifests.

Romans 15:13 AMP says,

13 "May the God of hope fill you with all joy and peace in believing [through the experience of your faith] that by the power of the Holy Spirit you will abound in hope and overflow with confidence in His promises.

Night **39** – Boast in Believing Without Reasoning

Many people, all over the world, get on planes every day. They take flight, trust the pilot, and have confidence that they will reach their destination without absolute proof that they are completely safe from harm. This is believing without reasoning. We believe in certain airlines. We believe in our favorite sport's athletes, or even our favorite political candidate, without reason.

However, when it comes to God, we tend to still need a reason to believe in one of his promises and accept its reliability. I believed God; except, I didn't believe he would perform miracles for me because I didn't deserve it. I challenged my own belief system. I noted one of the most famous bible stories ever, about Abraham and Sarah. God promised them a son in their old age. The amazing point of this story? God did it anyway; regardless of Sarah's unbelief.

Romans 4:19-20 AMP says,

19 Without becoming weak in faith he considered his own body, now as good as dead [for producing children] since he was about a hundred years old, and [he considered] the deadness of Sarah's womb.

20 "But he did not doubt or waver in unbelief concerning the promise of God, but he grew strong and empowered by faith, giving glory to God,"

<u>**Here's the lesson God gave me for Night 39:**</u>

Believing on his promise is not a matter of whether you deserve it. It's a matter of God's will, his plan, and purpose for your life.

Day 40 – Boast in a new "THINKING" regimen

Healthy confidence is worth fighting for. Fight to keep a healthy regimen for thinking. Make a habit to be conscious of how your thinking has affected your confidence level. Intentionally listen for twenty-four hours to understand the root of your thinking, then practice changing your thoughts. I literally guarded my own mind by watching every thought that took root in it. In doing this, I was able to take control of the renewal of my mind instead of accepting it as normal. A cluttered mind is not normal. A peaceful mind is natural. But, unfortunately, we won't know that until we renew our minds the right way. I learned on night 26 that to renew meant to make like new: restore to freshness, vigor or perfection. To Renew also means to give fresh strength to, or replace, or renovate something that is broken or worn out.

Psalms 94:19 AMP says,

19 When my anxious thoughts multiply within me; your comforts delight me."

Close your eyes for sixty seconds in peace. What does your mind's eye reveal? When I did this exercise, my mind definitely needed to a change for the better; cluttered it was!

Here's the lesson God gave me for Day 40:

The intent of God's word is to comfort my every thought. Be transformed or changed by accepting the comfort of his word. Be watchful and guard your thinking, then change it for the better.

Night 40 – Boast in appreciating your OWN Light

The first thing I did, during this process, was to educate myself on what confidence was. I needed to define this word "confidence" so that I could understand when and where I lost it. I found that confidence is a feeling of self-assurance arising from appreciation of one's own abilities or qualities. So basically, I didn't have self-assurance? Wow. This definition hit me like a ton of bricks. Why did I not appreciate myself? This feeling of self-assurance comes from appreciating my own abilities and qualities. Although, I didn't think I was the best at preaching, singing, or just doing ministry; surely, I should have some appreciation since I was doing God's work, right? God spoke to me. He said, Felicia, you love ministry and people; but you don't exactly see any self-worth in your calling or your own light the way you see it in others.

I really longed to understand this statement. It was so profound to me that I literally changed my thinking about myself. I wasn't proud of myself. Eureka! I finally understood! How could I better myself and my way of doing things or how I lived my life? How do I do life with self-assurance? Doing it to the point of where I could appreciate my own abilities was a major point that I'd never realized before.

Here's the lesson God gave me for Night 40:

Focusing on your abilities vs. good works will cause your light to dim; if not go out completely. Whatever your singular or plural uniqueness is, shine bright knowing that God your father will be glorified in heaven.

Your light is not to compete with anyone else. We shine together. Accept Jesus as your personal savior and turn your unique light on. He shines in us through our good works.

Matthew 5:16 KJV says,

16 "Let your light so shine before men, that they may see your good works, and glorify your Father which is in Heaven."

I'm so grateful to have found my light! With the leading of the Holy Spirit, I figured out how to appreciate it more than ever before! My light is as bright as the sun; just the way God intended it to be. No longer dimmed. I am an empathetic, unique, shining light. I served low self-esteem its final eviction to vacate my mind. I put God back on the throne of my mind!

In conclusion,

God affectionately said this to me concerning people with healthy self-esteem vs low self-esteem regarding confidence:

"Felicia, a conceited person with over-extended self-esteem, hypes up their view of themselves through the opinions of others. This influence causes them to put themselves on the throne of their own minds instead of me. Likewise, anyone with low self-esteem, having too little self-esteem, also have put themselves on the throne of their minds because they have centered their minds around the opinions of others. The person with too much self-esteem is equal to the one with low self-esteem; I am not on the throne of either of their minds."

God should be on the throne of your mind at all times…

Dear Patron,

Thank you for taking the time to read my journaling devotional! The dahlia flowers on the pages of this book represents my own transformation. One symbolism of this flower is confidence by uniqueness. It reminded me while writing this book that I was as unique as this flower. My willingness to be myself, undisputedly and authentically, is just as provocative as this flower! I want to encourage you to rest in the knowledge of God about who you are! Not just his promises to you; rest in the eternal knowledge about you. You were created as a unique representation of the image of God. Boast in this knowledge. You are authentically UNDISPUTED. Be confident. Be at peace. Accept the help of your creator.

May God bless your own journey towards confidence.

Let's pray...

Dear God,

I pray that the neighbor that has read this devotional will receive strength with exceeding revelation after following my testimonial journey away from low self-esteem. My hope is that this devotional will prove to have directional instructions for someone else's road to a much-needed epiphany towards wholeness and confidence while intentionally encountering my God through intimacy and relationship.

In Jesus name,
Amen.

with Grace & Love,
-Elder Felicia Grayer